The Freelancer Manifesto

11 Big Ideas to Stand Out and Thrive in the New Economy

Steve Roller

The Freelancer Manifesto

11 Big Ideas to Stand Out and Thrive in the New Economy

Big Ideas Publishing, LLC

Cover design by Authority Fusion, Inc. www.DougCrowe.com

Steve Roller photo (back cover) by Justice Media

Layout and publishing, Dwight Clough, DwightClough.com

Inspiration

This book is dedicated to Emida, the love of my life. Thanks for indulging me as I traipse off to distant lands to explore, think, and write. I'm glad we've done most of the trips together, and I look forward to many more. You've given me the world, and I intend to spend the rest of my days giving it back to you.

To Alex, Solomon, Sapphina, and Zaria, I love you with all my heart. I am continually amazed at your creative gifts, and I can't wait to see what each of you do with them.

To my dad, Wayne Roller. You instilled in me a disciplined work ethic as I grew up. Watching your devotion to your family, your work, your faith, and your running (with me in the 1980's) gave me a foundation that I carry with me to this day. I hope to be the same kind of father and someday, grandfather, that you are. Thanks, Dad.

To my mom, Judy Roller. You gave me a love for reading, writing, teaching, and traveling. I don't think I would have set off for Europe at age 22, married a girl from Nigeria at age 30, or become a writer at age 37 if it weren't for you. I watched you embrace other cultures with your years of teaching English as a Second Language, and I'm trying to do the same.

Finally, to my grandma, Delphine Schmitz, who turned 100 years old on April 25, 2017. As of this writing, she still lives on her own and is still going strong. At the age of 95, she became a published author herself when her article was printed in the Catholic Knights member magazine, proof that it's never too late to get started.

Contents

Foreword

I remember the day I realized I could no longer work for anyone else.

At the time, I was working as an Executive Assistant for the Managing Director of one of the biggest banks in the world. I loved my boss at the time. He let me do my own thing and he challenged me. One day I asked him a question that completely shook me.

"Is there anybody in this bank who is a Director and under the age of 30?"

He raised his eyebrows and looked at me with a puzzled face. "Of course not, Katya. In banking, you have to pay your dues. It took me 25 years to get to where I am. It's sad and I don't agree with it, but it will never change."

Really? No matter how skilled, how dedicated, and how much money I brought the bank…as a 23-year old, I had no chance whatsoever of becoming a Director in the next 15 years.

That day I made myself a promise that no matter what, I would find a way to capitalize on the internet and the service-based industry and get out of banking.

If you're holding this book, you know that feeling.

The feeling of "I can do things myself and make so much more money" or "I am sick of other people being in charge of my reality."

Today, as a Live Stream Marketing Strategist and Consultant, I make more money some months than I used to make in banking for an entire year.

I'm writing this from the beach on the beautiful island of Malta, and yes, life is better than it used to be. But I've also put much more time into building my own business than working in the corporate world. And there's probably been ten times more stress and tears.

Like Steve will show you in this book, there is a dark side to the whole concept of "freedom" and working for yourself. A Dark Side nobody wants to talk about.

Steve isn't like that, though. He is one of the real people who doesn't try to lure you in with his "multi-six-figure business strategies." He tells you what it really took to become one of the most highly sought copywriters. It wasn't easy.

Steve is more humble than you can imagine. He doesn't even realize how influential he is and how the Copywriter Cafe community he built from scratch is truly a one-of-a-kind place where he is adored and respected. That's how I met him.

I remember the day I fell in love with Steve's work. He had some naughty clients who hadn't paid their invoices on time, so he offered to forgive their outstanding dues if they bought him a Starbucks gift card.

I remember thinking…what a genius! He made it fun, he nudged them gently to pay up, and he got paid in coffee. Non-taxable coffee! (Hope the IRS isn't reading this.)

So when he asked me to write this Foreword, I said yes immediately.

Steve clearly understands people. And he understands the power of persuasion.

I had to learn those lessons the hard way. If you don't understand people and you don't work harder than the next freelancer…you have no chance of making good money on your own.

You have to outwork and outsmart in business if you want to be successful.

The Freelancer Manifesto will give you a lot of strategies and practical tips on how you can do that in a way that works for you, without killing yourself.

I happen to know a thing or two about this. The online entrepreneur industry coined me "the Live Stream Queen" and the go-to expert for all things Facebook Live, Periscope, and live video marketing. Entrepreneur magazine named me the top live video specialist. None of that was "accidental."

You have to be *brilliant* at what you do and be obsessed. It has to be the thing that fuels you and the thing you cannot stop doing.

I also listened to the market and developed something nobody has done before. I found a gap! (Steve takes you through a process in this book for how to find your own gap in the market).

You have to zig while other people zag. You have to look at what everyone else is doing and do the complete opposite.

Steve is a big believer in all of this. He'll show you how to build a business, and he's the type of person who will always be honest.

Our world is a small place and people talk. Do well and good things will happen to you.

Do me a favor. Join Steve's Copywriter Cafe Facebook Group and tag me in it (Katya Varbanova), so I know you read this.

And be open to learning from Steve. Your life will never be the same.

LiveStreamKatya

Katya Varbanova

Introduction

Freelancing is difficult

Don't let anyone tell you it's not.

When someone tells you, "It's easy," "Anyone can do it," or worse—"It will be fun," they're misleading you.

It's not at all easy. Most people can't do it. And it's not fun until you start making serious money, which usually takes a few years (and some people never get there).

There's a dark side of freelancing no one likes to talk about.

Marketers selling you programs and systems designed to help you live the freelance lifestyle certainly don't want to tell you about it.

If they did, it would put a big dent in their sales.

Other freelancers don't want to talk about the dark side of freelancing either. Why not? It's embarrassing to admit that your chosen lifestyle isn't working out like you planned.

The reason you hear the same freelance success stories trotted out over and over? Because they're so rare.

And the ones that *are* legitimate?

There's usually more to the story than they're letting on.

From the Dark to the Light

So what is this Dark Side of Freelancing?

And if freelancing isn't everything it's cracked up to be, why are so many people ditching their jobs and jumping into self-employment and freelancing?

The Dark Side of Freelancing is reality. *My* reality, as someone who's been a freelancer now for over 30 years. From 1986 to 2003 I was in direct sales, and I've been a copywriter since 2004.

I'm not making millions (yet), but I've carved out a very successful career in both sales and copywriting.

Along the way, I've discovered the dark under-belly of freelancing, stumbled and fumbled my way through the challenges (with help from others), and emerged victorious.

I work on my terms, spend time with my wife and four kids, live in a nice neighborhood, and make decent money.

I also travel a lot, and bring my work with me when I do. In fact, I wrote this book while on sabbatical in South America. Escaping an entire Wisconsin winter was a nice side bonus.

Lifestyle freedom, baby! It's more important to me than the money.

Both have been good, and life is good, but not easy. You'll have to work hard and work a lot to make it as a freelancer.

The Dark Side of Freelancing is also the reality of many other freelancers I know.

Writers, copywriters, content writers, graphic designers, website developers, entrepreneurs, travel writers, independent sales people, consultants, and coaches are all operating in this arena.

Are you ready to make your mark?

As founder of the Copywriter Café, a Facebook group of thousands of writers, copywriters, and entrepreneurs, and Café Writer, a paid membership community, I've had the chance to counsel and coach over 500 people one-on-one since 2011.

A lot of them have gone on to big success. But you'd be amazed what people tell you in a private setting. I've heard the good, the bad, and the ugly.

I won't be using names in my book, but I'll be describing situations so you know what you're getting into (or are already immersed in).

More important, I'll show you how to *overcome* the Dark Side of Freelancing.

That's what this book is all about!

The Freelancer Manifesto will give you answers if you...

- Are tired of working for "the man"
- Don't fit into the corporate lifestyle
- Want to be able to live life on your terms
- Like the idea of working for yourself
- Have a business of your own (or an idea for one) and want to make it more profitable
- Realize that good, salaried jobs are going away
- Have an independent streak and know that you'd rather not have a boss

In other words, if you want to work for yourself, build a business you can be proud of, and make good money in the process, you're in the right place.

Over the course of this book, in **21 chapters with easy-to-implement ideas** you're not hearing anywhere else, I will lay out a different way to approach the freelance lifestyle.

You're going to get 11 Big Ideas to overcome the Dark Side and stand out and thrive in the New Economy.

Follow along, keep an open mind to some contrarian ideas, and take action.

Use this as your Guide Book for creating the freelance lifestyle you deserve. It's there for the taking.

[Legal disclaimer: I am not an attorney or a CPA, and what follows does not constitute legal or professional advice. It's simply a way of operating that's worked well for me and others I've counseled. Please consult professional legal, financial, and tax advisers before you launch your freelance business.]

One more thing before we dive in…

Why I do what I do

A week before Christmas of 2009, Emida and my kids and I showed up on the doorstep of her mom's house in Benin City, Nigeria. It was 11:00 pm and the house was dark.

We had traveled from Madison to Chicago by bus, Chicago to Istanbul on Turkish Air, Istanbul to Lagos the next day, Lagos to Benin City by small plane, and then the most harrowing taxi ride through crazy night-time traffic that I've ever experienced.

For the rest of my life, I'll never forget the joy on her face when she opened the door and saw us standing there. Iye (what we called my mother-in-law) was blown away that we had finally made the trip, and couldn't believe we were actually there.

See, for eleven years after Emida and I got married, I wasn't able to arrange this trip. As an employee, I could never take off more than two weeks at a time. As a freelancer, I finally could, and I did.

I will be a freelancer of some kind for the rest of my life because now I operate on *my* terms.

When I want to travel somewhere, I do. When I want to visit people I care about, I do. I've been able to build a business, write books, see my kids grow up, and see the world, all while making good money, because of freelancing.

This is what drives me. I can't think of any better lifestyle, and I want this for you, too.

Part I: Reality: 11 Things No One Wants to Talk About

Chapter 1: The Gig Economy is Here to Stay

We're in for a freelance tsunami, and there's nothing we can do to stop it.

Will you ride the wave, watch it from the shore, or get toppled over by it?

According to the Bureau of Labor Statistics, as of May 2015, 15.5 million people in the U.S. were self-employed, an increase of roughly one million since May 2014. That number is expected to keep growing at a steady clip.

By 2020, an Intuit study estimates that more than 40% of the American workforce, or 60 million people, will be independent workers. Freelancers, contractors, and temporary employees.

It's called the "gig economy," a term coined at the height of the financial crisis in early 2009. Huge numbers of the newly unemployed made a living by gigging, or working several part-time jobs, wherever they could.

Surprisingly, 89% of Americans are still unfamiliar with the term "gig economy" said the Pew Research Center in May 2016.

Are they living in a cave?

My guess is that if you're reading this, you're not only familiar with the gig economy, you're *taking advantage* of it.

I hope so, because it's getting bigger.

And it's further separating the Haves and the Have Nots in the digital world.

Some recent headlines:

"Working in the Gig Economy is Both Desirable and Detestable" (Fortune.com)

"The Gig Economy is Ripping Out Floor Below Middle Class" (alternet.com)

"The Gig Economy is coming. You probably won't like it." (The Boston Globe)

"There's no more jobs in the new 'gig economy.'" (New York Post)

The news isn't all bad:

"The Gig Economy: The Force That Could Save the American Worker" (Wired)

"Exclusive: See How Big the Gig Economy Really Is" (Time)

"The Gig Economy is Great for the U.S. Economy" (realclearmarkets.com)

So, which is it? Good for us freelancers? Or bad?

Both.

I wouldn't be writing this book if it was all a bed of roses and sipping Mai Tai's on the beach with your laptop.

The good news about the Gig Economy and becoming a freelancer? Anyone can join in!

The bad news? Anyone can join in!

Let's recognize that the Gig Economy is here to stay, okay?

Assuming you aren't yet independently wealthy and you're going to need to work for the next 10, 20, or 30 years, you have a decision to make.

Join in or not?

You're reading *The Freelancer Manifesto*, so you're a step ahead of the game.

You're going to get the real facts about freelancing, and figure out the pitfalls to avoid.

More important, you're also going to get 11 Big Ideas to overcome these pitfalls (the Dark Side).

I have an idea. Kind of a radical idea.

Let's flip this freelancer model on its head.

Here's what I mean, and stay with me for 60 seconds...

This is all about supply and demand. I majored in Economics at the University of Wisconsin—Madison in the late 80's, and the principles of economics have kind of stayed with me.

Everything in business revolves around supply and demand.

Supply and demand dictates the price you can get for your services, whether or not you'll even have a viable business, and how long you'll be able to sustain any particular business model.

Let's say you're a freelance copywriter specializing in writing explainer video scripts. You're one of the few really good ones. You've made a name for yourself, and your copy gets results.

The big companies who contract out to you have you on an unofficial retainer. You write fast, so you're able to make decent money, about $400-500 per day when you're hustling.

But you're somewhat limited because they're getting the clients, not you. And now that other copywriters have heard about this sweet deal, there are a lot more explainer video script writers than even a couple years ago.

If you don't change your business model, maybe create your own full-production company and develop a marketing system to bring clients on board, your income potential will probably go down in the coming years. Maybe quicker.

Make sense?

Here's another example.

Jill took an online copywriting course and then hung out her shingle as a "freelance copywriter."

She was actually a pretty good copywriter for a beginner, but not such a good marketer.

So, like hundreds or thousands of other freelance copywriters, she started bidding on jobs at places like Upwork.

Nothing wrong with that, in fact, I got my start on Elance and hustled there for almost a year. I still have a client that originated there in February of 2010.

The problem with this approach?

Jill is standing in line with hundreds of other look-alike copywriters. She's going where there's lots of work, for sure. But the supply exceeds the demand.

There are more freelance copywriters looking for work there than clients hiring copywriters.

As such, it's a race to the bottom. In other words, in order to "get picked," copywriters under-bid each other.

And even though clients aren't always looking for the lowest price provider, it still becomes a low-rent district.

It's really a sad sight. Hundreds of copywriters, groveling at the feet of people who might need their services, virtually saying, "pick me, pick me!" in a weak voice.

Not all together different from going to a big job fair where 40-50 clients show up, looking for hot, new copywriting talent.

Meanwhile, the clients are outnumbered by the copywriters by almost ten to one, and they're not necessarily going to hire anyone new anyway. They have their own copywriters already, after all.

The online dating scene is similar, or so I've been told.

The typical guy signs up at eHarmony.com or Match.com and fills out his profile, like a copywriter jumping into the fray at Upwork, eager to get started.

I don't care how great your profile picture is or how your bio reads. The odds are stacked against you.

It's a numbers game, pure supply and demand. And little chance of really standing out.

(Aside—I've often thought about using my copywriting skills to help wayward romantics on these dating sites increase their odds for success. There's a free idea for you.)

Now, let's flip that freelancer model.

Instead of going straight to Upwork and competing with the masses, Jill decides to step back and brand herself as the Main Street Marketer.

Rather than going after all the clients everyone else is, Jill takes direct response marketing and packages it in a way that the average small, local business can understand and use.

Her target audience is any small to medium-sized business that spends a decent amount of money on advertising.

They don't have the budget to hire an ad agency or to have an in-house marketing team. They've never even thought of hiring a freelance copywriter, and may not even know what a copywriter is. (One reason to avoid the term.)

Think businesses that put a space ad in the Yellow Pages, a regular space ad in the local paper, or a spot on the local high school team's athletic poster (more as a donation than as an ad, of course).

They've spent money on Val-Pak, and digital marketing agencies are probably bombarding them (and confusing them) with promises of Facebook ad riches.

Tremendous opportunity here for Jill to play against all those things.

She's the Main Street Marketer who comes to their rescue.

See the difference? Upwork Jill versus Main Street Marketer Jill. No comparison.

Supply and demand, my friend.

Positioning. Branding. Standing out. Doing things different.

It takes a bit of a contrarian mindset.

Are you with me?

You're in for a wild ride.

I've got some more myths to expose, sacred cows to slay, and some downright untruths and marketing mischief to "out" first.

Before we get to the Light, I need to delve ever so briefly into the Dark Side.

If only so you know what to avoid, right?

Bottom line: the Gig Economy is here to stay.

You and I are going to be a part of it, along with probably 1.3 billion people all over this great planet of ours.

Let's make the most of it.

Let's stake our claim, build a true *business*, and flip this Gig Economy supply and demand model on its head.

Ready?

I have a few confessions to make first...

Chapter 2: Confessions of a (Formerly) Clueless Copywriter

On March 31, 2009, I took a serious leap of faith.

In the midst of the worst recession since the Great Depression, I quit a good-paying position with the largest bank in the Midwest.

I had four kids in school and a wife who was also a freelance creative type (she's a mural artist.)

So, yes, a writer and an artist with no discernible plans for steady income in the near future. One regular monthly client between the two of us. No benefits. Not a whole lot of savings.

Smart move, hey?

Our friends and family all felt sorry for us, and I think they were secretly plotting to take up a collection for us at Thanksgiving that year.

I'm happy to report that we didn't need it.

While I didn't hit the coveted six-figure mark in my first year, or my second, everything worked out quite well.

I made more in my first full year as a freelance copywriter than I had in the last year at my corporate job. This year I should triple it.

We took three weeks off in 2009 to visit my wife's family in Nigeria. We spent a month in Ecuador in the summer of 2011, and nine weeks there in 2014. Last year I went back for a Solo Sabbatical for ten weeks.

In the last eight years I've taken off about twelve months all together to travel. It's one of the main reasons I became a freelance copywriter.

I tell you all this because I truly believe that if I can make it big, you can, too.

Confession Time

See, I did it *in spite of* being pretty clueless, and I hope my experience lets you see that I'm a regular guy. I stumbled around and made a lot of mistakes, but figured out enough to make a decent living.

And I did it in an unorthodox way. You don't have to follow the mainstream advice. In fact, you probably *shouldn't* follow mainstream advice. It's aimed at the masses, and it's a cookie-cutter approach.

No matter what kind of freelancer you are, you'll understand what I'm talking about.

I'm a copywriter, and many of the examples I use throughout *The Freelancer Manifesto* relate to freelance copywriters.

But the same ideas apply to freelance graphic designers, website builders, ghost writers, bloggers, photographers, authors, translators, English teachers, virtual assistants, personal trainers, fitness instructors, developers, coders, musicians, tour guides, and travel writers.

If you've made up your mind that the corporate life is not for you, this book is for you. If you find cubicle land and conformity too stifling, this book is for you. And if you are determined to succeed as an entrepreneur, this book is most definitely for you.

Ready to dive in? Here are seven ideas to get started with, along with seven takeaways that will help you forge your own unique path:

1. I thought clients were going to come to me.

I really did. I thought all you had to do was take a copywriting course or read a few books, practice a bit, print up some business cards and slap a website up, and wait for the phone to start ringing.

Delusional, right? Just like when I was 12 years old and thought I was going to play Major League baseball someday.

In my industry of copywriting, I had heard about all these six-figure copywriters and just assumed I was going to magically become one, too, right away.

Maybe you've heard the same kind of success stories in your area of specialty. The thing is, for everyone you see who makes it big, there are probably ten or twenty who don't make it at all.

Well, here's the thing. Delusion is okay as long as it's eventually accompanied by some smart marketing strategies.

The first thing I did was tell everyone I knew who was a potential client that I was a copywriter (which I usually had to explain in layman's terms.)

And when they asked me, "Do you do _____?" (website copy, landing pages, brochures, email marketing, etc.), the answer was always, "Yes." I figured it out as I went along. As long as I knew more than the client and could help them increase sales, that's all that mattered.

Takeaway: You can be clueless about marketing, but make sure you pick at least one simple thing, and do it over and over again.

In my case, that one simple thing was keeping my eyes and ears open for potential business wherever I went, and not being afraid to ask leading questions.

2. I didn't pick a niche.

Most experts say that you need to specialize right from the start. "Nobody wants to work with a generalist" is the common reason given.

I agree. It's easier to get clients if you establish yourself in a particular niche.

The problem is that you're actually *not* an expert in the beginning, even if you give yourself that title (like a lot of people do these days.)

I could have called myself a financial copywriting expert because I was interested in that area. But when a client can choose from any *real* financial copywriting expert like Clayton Makepeace, John Forde, or Mike Palmer, I don't quite measure up.

What I did instead, and what I recommend you do, is *find a gap*. In other words, look for where you can position yourself in the marketplace. Figure out where you can apply your skills where there's actually a demand and perhaps not enough "supply."

For example, I think it's difficult to call yourself a natural health copywriter (even if you learned that niche quickly), call on a company like Rodale or Boardroom, which hires A-level copywriters, and get them to notice you or take a chance on you.

You could, however, call yourself a natural health copywriter, look for an upstart company online or a local health food store, and start writing copy tomorrow. Those type of businesses aren't getting hounded by copywriters who want to write for them.

In other words, *go where other freelancers aren't.*

If you're a photographer, go where the other photographers aren't. Weddings and babies? Crowded space, right? Maybe try corporate head shots or re-branding website photography.

The other way to "find a gap" is to find a niche where there is a potentially big demand, the companies in that niche hire freelancers, but most of those freelancers don't seem to be doing a stellar job. Or the companies try to do it themselves, without great results.

I found that a lot of small fitness studios and personal trainers fell into this category, so I worked with a few of them. I also worked with a variety of non-traditional copywriting clients who needed to grow, but didn't quite know how to do it, including a long-term care insurance company, a CPA, and a financial planner. I wrote copy for a life coach and a seminar company.

Takeaway: Find a gap. Instead of going after the big niches and the big companies that every freelancer would love to work for, go where there's a need but not a lot of freelancers.

I might have done very well if I had picked a niche right away, but I did just fine working for a variety of businesses in diverse areas, and you can, too.

3. I don't have any certifications or official credentials.

I've taken a few copywriting programs, but never finished one.

Can I fill you in on a little secret?

You'll probably never have a client ask you if you've finished any particular program or course of study. They also don't care what books you've read, what masters you've studied, or what professional organizations you belong to.

It's like employers asking me what my college grade point average was. It's never happened, and it doesn't really matter.

The only thing they care about is whether you can deliver results.

For us copywriters, can you write good copy that resonates with their readers and spurs them to take action and buy? That's it.

So when I felt I learned enough in a program to apply it to helping businesses grow, I stopped studying and started working.

I'm not saying you *shouldn't* finish a program. All I'm saying is you don't *have to*, and no one will ever ask you if you did.

Takeaway: Don't wait to get started. Too many freelancers drag their feet, taking one program after another, delaying the inevitable challenge of actually working for a client.

It's like a college student going on to grad school to get their Masters, then their PhD., then another degree, so that they don't have to put their skills and knowledge to the test in the marketplace.

Same thing with any freelance profession. Your credentials don't mean as much as what you can actually deliver. That being said, I did get some professional level of authority early on in the form of a celebrity testimonial. More on that later.

Learn a lot, soak up a lot, then apply it.

4. I hate getting up early and almost never do it anymore.

What does this have to do with freelancing, or success in general?

Gurus, A-level copywriters, coaches, and people who love to announce to the world that they get up at 4:59 A.M. every day of the year are always making me feel guilty that I'm not doing the same.

I read emails everyday from success experts that advocate the practice of getting an early start on the day. We all know Ben Franklin's "Early to bed, early to rise..."

I get it. I'm just not going to do it, and you don't have to either to be a successful freelancer.

Which leads me to another myth I'd like to dispel: *You're not going to be lazing around in your pajamas and slippers, working a couple hours in the morning while you drink your coffee, then heading to the beach to relax for the rest of the day!*

I only know two copywriters who operate this way and make really good money, and they're both a freak of nature. Maybe there are others out there, but the bottom line is that freelancing is hard work. Get the "laptop on the beach" picture out of your head.

Takeaway: You can work at whatever time of day you want, as long as you do the work and put in the time necessary to deliver good work.

It doesn't matter *when* you work, as long as you put the time in. You simply can't get around the fact that freelancing of any kind isn't a carefree walk in the park.

5. My family members, neighbors, and most of my friends have no idea what I do for a living, and I prefer it that way.

When I started out, however, I wanted everyone to know that I was a "copywriter." I thought it carried a certain amount of panache and prestige.

Then I realized that nobody knew what a copywriter was or what we did, and most people didn't really care.

I've come to the conclusion that I'm never going to be the rock star center of attention and conversation at cocktail parties. My friends who own successful companies are never going to be impressed with my writing gig. My relatives will never brag about me the way they would if I worked for a big company with a recognized name.

I'm okay with that, and I've made it my mission to keep a low profile, outside of copywriting circles, of course.

I like the fact that the neighbors can't figure out my schedule, because I come and go at odd hours of the day, and I travel frequently. It creates a certain air of mystery about you when no one knows what you do, but they see you living the good life.

What they don't see is that for six to eight hours a day, I'm buried in my office, pounding away at the keyboard. Or actually *working* for a couple hours a day at my second office, a local coffee shop, brainstorming Big Ideas.

Takeaway: Forget about impressing others. Calling yourself a "copywriter" probably won't cut it. Or "designer," "photographer," or any other freelance label.

So put your head down, work like crazy, and make it your mission to get people wondering how in the world you became successful by hanging around the house all day and not going to work.

Trust me, there's no point in trying to explain to most people what exactly you do, without a boss, an office, or a real title.

6. I've never sent out a self-promotional marketing piece or email, and I don't even have my own website search engine-optimized.

Yes, I think you should finish programs that you start, and yes, you should optimize your website and market yourself.

I just want you to know that it's not completely necessary.

This is another area freelancers get caught up on. You could spend weeks or months on your website, tweaking it until every single page and word is exactly right.

Better to get it mostly right and focus on delivering top-notch work for clients.

Speaking of, when you're first starting out, don't you *have to* do a major self-promotional marketing campaign?

Well, no.

You can, certainly.

The problem with that, like the website problem, is that new copywriters, new freelancers in general, tend to spend an inordinate amount of time creating and planning this monster marketing campaign.

I've seen writers agonize over this for months, even up to a year, because they're not sure if everything sounds right, or how to position themselves.

Why not just get started in a simple way?

Takeaway: Here's what I'd recommend. Start small with good old-fashioned local networking. As I said earlier, find a gap, then start small. Hang on to the clients you have, build them into bigger clients, and get referrals from them.

Think about this. What's going to pay the bills? Working for whatever clients you can get, or getting bogged down in creating the perfect website and self-promotional marketing campaign?

Focus on making money in the beginning with a website that's at least 80% right, and worry about everything else later.

7. My biggest fear in life (besides the fear of losing my hair and my teeth) is that I won't leave my mark on the world

That fear is one of the driving forces behind my desire to be a well-respected copywriter, a best-selling author, and a highly-regarded public speaker.

It's what motivates me to get up in the morning (just not at 4:59 A.M.) and press on.

If you ever read the classic self-help book by M. Scott Peck, *The Road Less Traveled*, you know what the first line of the book is: *"Life is difficult."*

Well, I have news for you: *Freelancing is difficult.*

You probably won't make six figures your first year, or your second.

If you think it's easier working for yourself than for an employer, think again. If you think clients are going to come to you because you took a course or went to a conference, go back and read confession number one above.

Freelancing is difficult, and I believe there's one thing above all that will get you through the tough learning period of the first few years. In addition to being extremely disciplined and becoming a good at your craft...

You need to have a strong emotional purpose for what you're doing.

Wanting to make six figures isn't an emotional purpose. Wanting to buy your 80-year old parents a house in Florida is.

Paying off your debt or being your own boss could be emotional purposes, but you might want to tie them to something more inspirational and big.

Takeaway: Develop your own strong emotional purpose for wanting to become a successful freelancer. Something beyond making a lot of money or firing your boss. Do this, and you'll greatly increase your chances of making it happen.

Mine? I have quite a few. I want to take my wife to Israel for our 20th anniversary next year, and a trip around the world for our 25th. I want to live abroad for a year before my kids are out of school.

Those things take time freedom and location freedom, which freelancing affords. That's a big reason I do what I do.

More than anything, I want to leave my mark on the world, and I believe beyond any doubt that I'll do it through writing, creating, and speaking.

I want my kids, and, down the road, my grandkids, to know that I made it big and gave them everything I could, and that I made a difference.

If your goal is to make it big and make a difference, I hope these seven confessions and seven takeaways help.

We're just getting warmed up, and the rest of *The Freelancer Manifesto* will be your roadmap to making the freelance lifestyle work for you.

First, a few things you'll want to avoid that no one else is telling you…

Chapter 3: Don't be the Willy Loman of Freelancing

The original title of this book was "Death of a Freelancer." A little dark, hey?

It was a play on words on *Death of a Salesman*, Arthur Miller's 1949 play. If you're not familiar with it, Willy Loman is a traveling salesman who's seen better days. He relied heavily on his personality in his younger days, and it's not working so well for him anymore. He's struggling to keep up with changing times, and plagued with self-doubt about his place in the world. A large part of his identity and self-worth is tied up in his work.

A lot of freelancers I see are in a similar predicament.

In Willy Loman's day, the American Dream was a good corporate job, a house in the suburbs, and a comfortable retirement. The American Dream for many freelancers today is to work for themselves, not a corporation, location independence versus a place to commute to every day, and enjoying travel and typical retirement luxuries *now*, not waiting for some far-off or never-happening retirement.

In Willy Loman's case, he got left behind. He outlived his usefulness, lost his youthful enthusiasm, and sunk into a serious depression.

In the case of many freelancers I see, it's not so much a case of getting left behind. It's more a situation where they never quite find their place in the freelancing world to start with. Let's face it, the barriers to entry are extremely low, so anyone can jump in and test the waters. Put up a website, and you're in business.

Only problem, it's not so easy.

I've talked to hundreds, maybe thousands of freelancers who struggled until they started applying the principles in this book. They were sold a bill of goods about how great it is to work for yourself. And they suffered silently while barely making as much as they did at their job, with a whole lot more expenses. Over time, it can wear on you and beat you down.

Let it go too long, and you might just fade out like our protagonist friend in *Death of a Salesman*.

I saw it in direct selling from 1986-2003, and I've seen it in the freelance copywriting world I've been a part of since 2004.

Why is that? A few reasons:

1. People don't know what they're getting into (one of my purposes in writing this book).

2. People don't realize any business, and especially any type of freelancing, involves selling. There's a negative connotation with selling that isn't justified.

3. Lack of patience, along with no sense of urgency. What I mean is, in the beginning, they think it's going to happen instantly. When they don't make good money quickly, they get frustrated.

4. At the same time, they also don't have a sense of urgency about changing their circumstances. They think it will happen naturally, as if the longer they freelance, the more money they deserve to make. So they don't put in massive effort, and they keep coasting along.

5. They run out of money.

6. Their skills aren't good enough.

Those are the six main reasons why freelancers either quit or eke out an average living.

Don't be that freelancer! Don't be the Willy Loman of Free-lancing!

Before you get too deep into the Wild West land of the New Economy, take a step back. Reading this book is a good first step, or a good do-over if you're already freelancing and haven't made your first million yet.

Re-think what you've been told about working for yourself. Question the status quo, and the gurus and experts trying to sell you on one course after another. Maybe all you need is a $15 book and a new way of operating.

I believe freelancing, and the logical extension, building a true business (which we'll talk about more in Chapter 14), is a noble calling.

I believe that freelancers add tremendous value to the economy. In fact, I would say freelancers *drive* the economy.

Freelancers are filling the gaps left by corporate downsizing and reshuffling, and provide extremely efficient business solutions.

There are millions of freelancers out there hustling, keeping the wheels of industry turning, as Zig Ziglar used to say about salespeople. It applies equally well here.

I'll elaborate on this in Chapter 5. And Part II has 11 chapters telling you how to overcome this "dark side" of freelancing.

Before I get to the practical, action-oriented solutions, let me make a quick side-step. Let's look at how mindset and self-confidence is a huge predictor of future success in freelancing.

You need solid, foundational, **"hard" skills** to make it big as a freelancer:

Connecting

In the New Economy, this is a combination of social media skills, good old fashioned networking, meeting with people over coffee (still my favorite way to connect), making business connections wherever you go—online and off, and simply making friends. Yes, that's a skill.

Marketing

You need to understand marketing systems. Random campaigns or sporadic attempts won't cut it. One of the best and easiest ways? Build a list through valuable content, then stay connected with your audience on a regular basis.

Selling

I believe selling is just as important today as ever. Even with the best marketing and copywriting, you will have to communicate with clients and prospects by phone or in person at some point.

And the final hard skill every business person needs to get good at...

Copywriting

I founded the Copywriter Café, so yes, I'm a bit biased. And as you can see from this book so far, most of my examples of freelancing pertain to copywriters.

That's because copywriting is *the* foundational skill upon which all others are built. Whether you're a graphic designer, content writer, photographer, or any other type of freelancer, you should have some foundational knowledge of and talent for copywriting. No matter what marketing system you use, you have to communicate effectively. And if you understand copywriting, you understand your audience.

Some would argue that marketing trumps copywriting. In other words, your message can be so-so, but if everything else is in place, you'll still build a business. Probably true, but why not have good marketing *and* good copywriting? It will give you a much better overall image, which goes a long way toward getting bigger.

My suggestion? Work on each of them, consistently, simultaneously.

Soft skills

Now, I would argue that **"soft" skills** matter even more.

Don't worry. I'm not going to go all "Law of Attraction" on you here. Nothing of the sort. And I'm definitely not talking about developing a "positive mental attitude."

I don't subscribe to either of those philosophies. You couldn't pay me to read a book or listen to a podcast on that stuff.

This is different.

You've heard of IQ (Intelligence Quotient), which is meant to measure a person's intelligence or reasoning abilities (measured using problem-solving tests). It's controversial, not necessarily accurate or fair, and not a good overall predictor of success.

EQ, or Emotional Quotient, looks at a person's emotional intelligence, which refers to how well we handle ourselves and our relationships. There are four components: self-awareness, self-management, empathy, and social skills. The concept was popularized by Daniel Goleman with his 1995 book, *Emotional Intelligence: Why It Can Matter More Than IQ.*

Well, I've developed a test that I call FQ™, or Freelance Quotient™. It's a test that measures your potential to make it as a freelancer.

I'll go so far as to say that every aspiring freelancer of any kind —writer, copywriter, web designer, graphic designer, etc.— should take this test *before* jumping into the abyss of freelancing.

Finding out your FQ™ could save you thousands of dollars misspent on programs, coaching, and conferences. Tens of thousands maybe. You can take the actual quiz at freelance-quiz.com or freelancequotient.com. (Both go to the same page.) I'll give you the condensed version here…

If you're going to have a successful freelance career, there are four main "soft skills" you need to have—the "FQ™ Four."

Can you develop these skills? I'll let you think about it first, then I'll give you my thoughts at the end of this chapter.

The FQ™ Four

Among many other things, if you're going to succeed as a freelancer, you need to have:

1. An abundance mindset

Do you really want to become wealthy? Do you have a positive view of wealthy people and how they got there? Do you have an inquisitive view of the rich, rather than the more common covetous attitude toward them?

2. An entrepreneurial spirit

Do you have the drive to do things on your own? A sense of rugged individualism? Do you have a track record of success doing things by yourself, outside of an employee or team situation?

3. Style

This one is a little hard to explain. Running your own show requires a bit of style. More than if you're an employee working for someone else.

You need a confident, successful image. Poise. A sharp appearance, in person and online. A strong Personal Brand that isn't forced.

Aside from business, do you stand out? Do people listen to what you have to say? Do you follow the trends and blend in, or do you carve out your own path?

You need self-confidence that really only comes from past successes.

This is something I rarely hear anyone touch on. I see so many people jump into the fray, trying to be a freelancer or run their own business because they're tired of the 9-to-5 grind. They don't want to work for a boss anymore. They want to do their own thing.

But they've never really *done* their own thing. Maybe they've been a great employee and done fantastic working for someone else. That's different than working for yourself. Way different. Do you have a track record of success where you've worked completely independently and been successful?

Have you ever been in sales? Not just been *in* sales, but *successful* at it?

If not, what makes you think you'll be able to sell yourself and your services? Being in business requires more than good marketing. You need to *sell*, and people who can do this also seem to have *style*. They often go hand-in-hand.

If you're not sure, you may want to reconsider freelancing. Starting up your own business requires a lot more than knowledge from a course or program. It requires an abundance mindset, an entrepreneurial spirit, style, and...

4. Resilience

Are you open to trying new ideas, even if they might fail? Are you open to constructive feedback, yet immune to harsh criticism? Do you have bounce-back-ability? (My made-up word for this chapter.) You'll need it. Things don't always work out on the first try.

This is another area where sales people have an upper hand. Sales people are used to dealing with criticism and rejection, and they don't take it personally.

Again, like my questions above about style, do you have a track record of resiliency? If you do, great. Apply that same level of persistence and stick-to-itiveness (one of my favorite words) to your new freelance endeavors and you'll have a much better chance of success.

There you go. The four "soft skills" that are at the core of your FQ™ (Freelance Quotient™) score. The actual test at freelancequiz.com goes into much more detail, but for now, rate yourself from 1-5 on each, 1 being low and 5 being high. Be brutally honest with yourself.

If you scored between 4-8, you might want to consider NOT going into business for yourself. If you already are, and you're committed to it, realize you've got a lot of work to do.

A 9-14 score is average. You should be fine, but recognize that you still have room for improvement. It's an ongoing process. You might want to consider getting a mentor or coach, not for the business side of things, but for your mindset and brand.

15-20? You're probably already cranking, and should keep doing what you're doing. If you have a high score in this range and you're *not* doing well, it's not head issues getting in the way. You probably just need to get your business systems and processes squared away.

How did you fare?

If it wasn't at least a 9, do you think you could work on those "soft" skills? Could you get them to the point where you'd need to in order to become a successful freelancer?

Do you want the freelance lifestyle enough to do that?

Can you develop these skills? Yes…and no.

I think it's extremely hard to overcome past baggage and hang-ups about rich people. If you have a cynical view of them, you'll be fighting an internal struggle. Having negative attitudes about money, wealth, and rich people will almost guarantee that you won't become one of the rich yourself.

You almost have to disassociate yourself from others who do have negative attitudes about wealth. Even if it's family or friends, if you want to succeed in business on your own, you should probably limit your time with them.

Entrepreneurial spirit? Also very hard to overcome. If you've been used to getting a regular paycheck most of your life, and haven't had to sell on straight commission or get paid based only on results, this one may be tough to deal with.

You need a seriously hungry desire to do your own thing, and a competitive streak, if you're going to make it as a freelancer.

Can you work on your style? Absolutely. Get help from someone on this—a mindset coach, a mentor, a branding specialist. If you need a recommendation, I know some good people.

Can you work on your resilience? Yes. Same thing, you'll want to get help from someone. Don't attempt to do this all on your own.

One of the reasons I created the Copywriter Café was to give people a place to come together and help each other on these things. Started in 2012, we're still going strong, and it's considered one of the most useful, helpful, and friendly groups of its kind on Facebook. If you want to check it out, just add your name here and I'll approve you:

https://www.facebook.com/groups/CopywriterCafe/

If you're open to working on these things, with the right help you can develop an abundance mindset and entrepreneurial spirit.

It's rare, though, and I really only think 10% of the population is cut out for being a freelancer or entrepreneur of any type. Considering the statistics from Chapter 1, that up to 40% of the workforce will be some type of freelancer by the year 2020, that's a big gap.

My hope is that this book will actually *discourage* and *dissuade* some people from pursuing this path, and save you thousands of hours of time and tens of thousands of dollars.

See what I did? You spent $15 for a book, and I'm saving you tons of time and money.

Now, if you're still here, excellent! You're in the rare 10% of people who *should* be freelancing, and you'll probably be successful at it. *Wildly* successful if you put the ideas in this book into action. And that's when the fun begins…the lifestyle, freedom, money, travel, recognition, all on *your* terms.

Let me take a step back here.

I've been painting a bleak picture so you can get the truth about freelancing. Most books and programs for showing freelancers how to do it are the opposite.

They go on and on about the glamorous "laptop-on-the-beach lifestyle" or "digital nomad" life you'll soon have, working a couple hours in the morning, then spending the rest of the day golfing, going to the beach, or seeing the sights of Europe while your hapless friends back home grow more envious by the day.

That's not realistic for 99.8% of freelancers, and I'm not going to insult your intelligence by even remotely hinting at that scene.

I know of only two freelancers (copywriters) who ever claimed to have that kind of schedule. And there's a back story to both.

But I do want to remind you here that freelancing is a wonderful way to make a living! You live life on your terms, you can work from anywhere, and the money *can* be very good…IF you set it up right from the beginning. Build a solid foundation. Be patient. Don't follow the crowd.

It's worked for me, and it can work for you.

So I've spent most of this chapter telling you *not* to be the Willy Loman of Freelancing. That you better have a fairly high

FQ™. And that besides the "hard skills," these FQ™ "soft skills" better be present as well.

Let's say you have all that and you're still here reading, and you've decided, "Yes! I'm in."

Do you want the one other factor that will give you an edge on your freelancing peers?

Emotional purpose

Have a powerful **emotional purpose** for doing what you do. Your deeper **reason why**. Wanting money isn't enough. We all want money, and after a while, the allure of more money fails to motivate.

The key is to attach a greater purpose to what you're doing.

Mine?

1. Travel. For myself, but even more, to give travel opportunities to my family.

The big reason I became a full-time freelancer in 2009 after being in sales and the corporate world for 23 years was to be able to do more extended travel.

Working for an employer, I was never able to get off enough time to see my wife's homeland of Nigeria. In December of 2009, we finally went there, and it's one of the highlights of my life. I've been to Ecuador three different times for a total of 23 weeks so far, with and without my wife and kids. You'll hear more about this in my next book: *The Solo Sabbatical: How to increase your health, wealth, and relationships by getting away from it all.*

In 2019 or 2020, I'm planning a big Café World Tour, traveling all over the world for a good part of the year to meet as many of my Café Writer members as possible, in person. Beyond that? I plan to split my time 50/50 between the States and South America. As a writer, I can do that.

In my mind, there is no better way to spend your time and money than traveling.

2. Help 1,000 freelancers over 10 years build a profitable business.

This was my original purpose when I started the Copywriter Café. I've had an impact on more than that many by now, considering we have over 6,400 members, and have had a direct influence on a few hundred through one-on-one coaching and my retreats.

My point is, **have a cause bigger than yourself.**

I know freelancers who attach their business to a worthy cause, donating 5 or 10% of their profits to a charitable organization they feel strongly about. You don't have to give money, but get involved.

Not only does it make people want to work with you more, but it will give you a sense of purpose beyond your own personal gain. Whether it's working toward clean drinking water in a developing country, fighting sex trafficking internationally, or giving to the local Humane Society, if you can find a cause to get involved with and align your business with, you'll have a richer life as a result.

3. Leave something behind.

I go into this a lot more in Chapter 16, Leave a Legacy. We're just passing through, and I can't imagine only wanting success and material gain in this world. I want to leave something meaningful behind, to know that somehow I made a difference in this world. I'm starting with writing books, and this is the first of many.

Generations from now, no one will read my social media posts, see my videos, or listen to my audio books. But they might pick up one of my books off the shelf and read it.

I plan to write a book a year for the rest of my life, and I have big plans for getting them into the hands of as many people as possible. The single best way I know of to leave a legacy is to write a book. If you have any desire to write one, let's talk. I might be able to help you.

4. Prove people right.

Some people say it's a motivating factor to prove their detractors wrong. For me, I never really had detractors. Most people believe in me more than I believed in myself.

As a result, I want to prove my *supporters* right!

I thank 21 people in this book, and there are probably a hundred more who've supported me along the way. It's a strong emotional purpose for me to want to prove that they were right for believing in me. I owe it to them, and I owe it to myself.

Think about the places you want to see, people you want to help, organizations you want to help, ideas you want to leave behind, or people you want to thank. Come up with your own powerful, personal emotional purposes for doing what you do, and you'll have a much better shot at making it than if your only goal is big money.

And it's a paradox, but when you take your eyes off the money and focus on other things, the money usually happens as a natural byproduct.

Mark it up

By the way, before we go any further: Write in this book! Mark it up. Take notes. Use it to trigger new ideas!

One of the reasons I put this in hard copy is because I love writing in books myself! It's much easier to go back and skim my notes than to re-read parts of a book, even if it's highlighted (which I don't do).

My intention is for this book to be a field manual of sorts, guiding you forward as you build your business in the coming years. I hope you take a lot of notes, and I hope you refer back to it often.

Now, on to the cows...

Chapter 4: Slaying the Sacred Cows

Every business has its "sacred cows." Those beliefs about business that the old-timers perpetuate, naïve newcomers are presented with as fact, and ambitious movers and shakers come up against.

They're often based partly on truth, but maintaining that belief system has long overstayed its practical use. By the way, a figurative sacred cow is a person or thing immune from questioning or criticism. The first use in English was in the mid-19th century, and became a common expression around 1905.

Let me give you a few examples from the corporate and sales worlds that I come from. It will give you a better idea of what I'm talking about.

Then I'll give you the seven "Sacred Cows" that I experienced coming into the freelance copywriter world. Seven sacred cows that still prevail. If you're not aware of the false logic behind them, they could hold you back.

So, before I talk about slaying the sacred cows of freelancing, there are two other arenas where the same mentality exists.

In the corporate world, you've heard the saying, "climb the corporate ladder," right? It implies that you start at the bottom, and little by little, you gain experience, earn promotions, and by golly, if you're lucky, after 25-30 years, you might just make Vice President.

Obviously, that's an outdated example since no one stays 25-30 years at a company anymore. But from post-World War II through the 80's and 90's, this was the case. "Climbing the corporate ladder," "paying your dues," and "company loyalty" were sacred cows.

Said whom? Said the guys running the company who wanted loyalty to them, of course. Said middle managers who *did* work their way up the company ladder for many years. They weren't about to let some hotshot young buck with big aspirations leap-frog the system.

Then along came the internet boom in the late 90's and early 2000's. It was almost a counter-culture opportunity opposite extreme to the buttoned-down, Wall Street corporate style that preceded it.

Gone was the sacred cow that you had to pay your dues. Gone was the idea of climbing the corporate ladder.

Ideas and ingenuity were in! Youthful exuberance was in! Old and stuffy were out! 40-year company retirement parties were out.

What mattered now was the ability to move fast, to come up with the next great domain name (think pets.com, which later went bust, of course), and implement the latest and greatest technical wizardry, to grab your share of the internet's new Wild West.

Still, even this new revolutionary start-up culture had its own sacred cows.

"All that matters is eyeballs." In other words, all you have to do is get people to look at your site! Sales? Whatever.

"A generic one-word domain name is key." Well, pets.com didn't work. Neither did food.com or a thousand others. But back in 1998, you didn't dare question the thinking of the day.

"People will switch their buying habits because…it's the inter-net!" (No business plan, just "hey, we're online, baby!")

You know what? Someone should have written *Death of an Internet Start-Up* in 1999, a precursor to *The Freelancer Manifesto*. We could have warned all those pie-in-the-sky dreamers of the pitfalls no one else warned them about.

It would have prevented the loss of billions of dollars, including money from a lot of everyday people on the sidelines who invested in those companies, even if they weren't on the payroll within the company.

This book is your guide to avoid a freelancing death like the internet stock bubble of 1999.

Read, absorb, pay heed, and ACT. *You* will prosper, while others fall by the wayside like a modern-day version of pets.com.

So those were three sacred cows that nobody thought to question in the heady days of the internet gold rush. If they had, maybe it would have ended differently.

Today, **there are seven sacred cows that I see in the freelance world**. I don't see anyone questioning them, or *slaying them* all together.

I am.

Keep in mind, this comes from my experience as a part-time freelancer from 2004-2008, and a full-time freelancer from March of 2009 to the present.

It also comes from coaching over 400 freelance copywriters one-on-one since 2011, and as the founder of the Copywriter Café in 2012.

The Copywriter Café group on Facebook has over 6,400 people as of August 2017, and is growing daily. CafeWriter.com is the fastest-growing copywriting paid membership site online.

I started both the group and the membership site because I wanted copywriters to see what they were getting into. In the beginning, in August of 2012, I wasn't trying to sell anything.

My main purpose was to form a lively, friendly community of copywriters who would always be there to help each other with ideas, advice, encouragement, and feedback. We weren't trying to sell a copywriting program or offer a pipe dream of writing barefoot on the beach, tapping away on a laptop for a few hours a day and making six figures.

The Copywriter Café was always a voice of reason, and one of my goals was to expose the myths of the freelance copywriting world!

By the way, the Copywriter Café Facebook group welcomes *any* freelancer who wants to build a business. We have authors who want to learn to sell more books, life coaches who need more clients, web designers who need a better marketing system, bloggers who are trying to build an audience, and internet marketers who need more sales. The common denominator? Copywriting, "selling in print or online," drives all of it.

Go to Facebook.com/groups/CopywriterCafe/ to check us out.

Warning: there's going to be some blood-shedding ahead. Let the slaying begin...

The Seven Sacred Cows of the Freelance Copywriting World (and the freelance world in general):

Sacred Cow #1

"Anyone can do it."

I found out about copywriting in July of 2004. I was surfing the internet, and came across an amazing little ad with this headline: *"Can you write a letter like this one?"*

Brilliant ad! It drew me in, and continued:

"Answer 'yes' and you'll never have to worry about your job or rely on others for your livelihood…

Instead, you will be in big demand, earning great money, writing a few hours a day from anywhere in the world you choose to live."

It was written by a copywriter I have huge respect for, and it's been a phenomenal success.

A little more context before I slay the "Anyone can do it" sacred cow. This promotion for a copywriting program (a great program, by the way), continues with these sub-headlines:

"Need $20,000? Write a couple letters"

"$160,000 from one letter"

"You can make between $80,000 and $540,000 per year"

Yowza! Who wouldn't want that!?

I did, I signed up for the program, and that was the start of my copywriting journey, which has turned out quite well.

The implication, however, is that it's really easy to make six figures per year as a freelance copywriter.

Is that possible? Can a freelancer of any kind make six figures? Of course. If you have talent and really work at it, 3-5 years is a realistic time frame to achieve this lauded benchmark (which in today's economy, really isn't very much money).

I know a handful of copywriters personally who have done it in their first year. A handful out of thousands of copywriters I know of in my group. Same goes for other freelance positions —graphic designers, website developers, travel writers, photographers.

My point: **it's not typical, and it's not easy**.

Six figures should be a baseline, not the be-all, end-all. It's a starting point. After taxes and expenses, $100,000 a year in the

States is about $5,000 a month. For most people, that's paying the bills. Nothing inspiring about that.

It's not easy, and not everyone can do it. A lot of people should NOT pursue freelancing, for various reasons we'll get into in Part I.

That's the first Sacred Cow: **"Anyone can do it."**

No, they can't! It's not easy, most people *won't* make six figures at it, and a lot of people shouldn't even try. Save your money. Skip the $400 online program or $1,500 conference to learn how to be a copywriter (and this is coming from someone who offers a $1,500 retreat myself).

Take a quiz at FreelanceQuiz.com to see if freelancing makes sense for you or not. It may not even be in your DNA, and I might have just saved you thousands of dollars and years of wasted effort.

Now, if it IS in your makeup, and you don't want to work for "the man" or any boss anymore, and you want to build a profitable business of your own, keep reading.

Sacred Cow #2

"You have to pay your dues."

Hogwash. If you want to burst on the scene as a freelance copywriter, graphic designer, web developer, travel writer, translator, or anything else, *have at it!* Go for it.

There's absolutely nothing that says you have to start at the bottom and work your way up.

If you have the skills, the confidence, and the personality or charisma to break in and quickly make a name for yourself, you should.

You know who *doesn't* think you should? The old-timers. The wizened veterans who *did* pay their dues. They paid their dues, finally made it to a respectable, profitable level, and they see *you* as a threat.

Regardless of age, in any given field, those who have been around for a while tend to resent the newcomers. You're competition!

You're also not jaded like they are. You have more youthful exuberance. If you're of a younger generation, you might very well be more adept at using technology than they are. You're probably more open to new changes, and quicker to make needed changes to adapt to the marketplace.

If you're anything like I was as a new freelancer, you're probably also a lot *hungrier*. You haven't made your first million yet. But you're determined to do so.

Are you starting to see where all these characteristics could be intimidating to freelancers who've been in your field for a while? They'd much rather you take your sweet time learning the ropes. Ha! Maybe even buy some of their programs to learn how to do it, or come to one of their conferences.

They'll probably lay out their "playbook" and give you all the surface-level nuggets to build your freelance business. They might even give you a "toolkit" of all their templates and forms (most of which are outdated and not suitable to your freelance business today).

There's a built-in incentive to perpetuate the myth of "paying your dues." It's in the best interests of everyone in that business who came before you. Don't fall for it.

If it sounds like I have a bit of a grudge against the status quo and these sacred cows of "six-figures is easy" and "you have to pay your dues," I really don't. I figured it out early on, so I never fell hard for it.

I slayed the "pay your dues" sacred cow, and you should, too. Ignore it, laugh at it, and snuff it out.

Fall victim to the "pay your dues" mentality and you'll die the slow death of a freelancer. There's no time for that.

Use the ideas in this book to succeed wildly, and celebrate the fact that we're in a whole new world. This is the Gig Economy, where anybody with the right amount of talent and chutzpah can make it. "Pay your dues" is a 20th-century mindset. Leave it there. Next…

Sacred Cow #3

"You need a substantial portfolio"

This one goes hand-in-hand with "pay your dues."

Whether you're a freelance graphic designer, photographer, or copywriter, people will want to see your work, right?

They want to see what you've done for others and what you can do for them. Makes sense, of course. We're all the same. If you're spending money, you want to know that the person you're hiring will get the job done.

Problem is, it's a Catch-22. You need a portfolio to get clients. But you can't build a portfolio without clients. Or can you?

Well, actually, you *can*. More on this in a minute. But first, do you really need to show a huge body of work to a prospect to get them to hire you? Not at all.

I would suggest that all you need is *one good example* of what you've done to get someone to hire you.

One good piece is all most prospects are going to look at anyway, and one project will lead to the next client. It's only a challenge when you're first starting out or when you've only

63

had one good project. After that, the rest of your career, it's a moot point.

So why is this a sacred cow? Because like the "pay your dues" sacred cow, it's one of those things perpetuated by those who came before you. They feel like they *have* paid their dues. They have built up a big portfolio of work. And *you*, my friend, rising up out of seemingly nowhere, are *the competition*!

They've worked hard to get where they are. The last thing they want is more competition from some green freelancer new on the scene.

The truth?

You *don't* need a substantial portfolio to get started. If you did, there wouldn't be thousands of new freelancers entering your field every year.

Here's what you DO need:

* **A specific solution to a problem**

You're going to hear me talk about this again and again. No matter what your freelance specialty, more than thinking of yourself as a copywriter or designer or whatever you are, think of yourself (and present yourself to clients) as a **problem solver** and an Idea Generator. (More on that in Chapter 7. Lots more.)

I always tell my coaching clients to package their services in a way that solves a specific problem.

For example, my friend, Jeff Melvin, helps businesses solve the problem of website visitors who don't buy. What's his solution? He helps them build their email list.

I wrote about this idea at length in *47 Ways to Do Copywriting*, a book available to my Café Writer Members only at this point, on Amazon soon.

- **One good portfolio piece**

Yes, only one. Most clients only need to see one example of what you've done for someone else in a similar situation as them. If you have to, work for free ONCE for the sole purpose of getting a good sample to show. If you're any good at what you do, someone will jump at the chance to let you work for them for free. Make sure you a good testimonial out of it, too, of course.

- **A big list**

A big list of prospective clients, that is, and I don't mean a list you rent or buy. I mean one you create, from scratch, without even having to spend any money.

- **A marketing plan**

This doesn't have to be complicated either. I'm not talking about huge marketing "funnels" or hiring specialists. We'll talk more about a list and a marketing plan later in the book.

And finally…

- **Hustle!**

And I mean that in every good sense of the word.

Sacred Cow #4

"You have to focus on a particular niche"

The logic says, "You can't be a generalist. If you're going to make it as a freelancer, you have to specialize."

And the accompanying analogy: A general practitioner medical doctor makes okay money. A cardiovascular surgeon makes really good money.

It's somewhat true, but overall a bad analogy. We're not medical doctors. We didn't go to 17 years of school plus eight years of residency.

I'm not saying you should be a jack-of-all-trades. But a lot of copywriters think you absolutely have to pick a niche.

The fact is, there isn't that much you need to learn about any particular niche. You could learn everything you need to know about the pet world, at least enough to write good copy for it, in 30 days.

This isn't medical school training to become a cardiovascular surgeon. **This is about learning the art of persuasion, known as copywriting. And those skills transfer from one niche to another quite well**.

If you can solve people's problems with your skills, whether you're a freelance graphic designer, website developer, or content marketing writer, why limit it to one niche? You solve problems, right? Help everyone if you can!

So why is this a sacred cow, and what's the solution? It's a sacred cow because it's *all* I ever heard when I first started freelancing. "You have to pick a niche" was the mantra perpetrated by…wait for it…people selling you a program on How to Pick a Niche. Imagine that.

Look, picking a niche can be a good way to go. If you have expertise in a certain area, by all means, go for it. You don't need a program to show you how to pick a niche. Love dogs? Does the prospect of working with dog trainers, breeders, or dog food manufacturers excite you? Well, copywriting for the dog industry sounds logical, right?

Guess what? You're still competing with hundreds of other dog or pet copywriters who also had the same idea. **You still have to stand out**.

Or let's say you're a graphic designer. You hear "pick a niche" and decide to focus on start-up tech companies. That's fine, but being defined by the audience you serve isn't necessarily the best way to stand out.

Better to be known for the *service* you provide and *how* you provide it (your process) than whom you serve. Perhaps best? Do all three. Specialize in a niche, become known for a particular service, and define your process.

The point is, you don't have to pick a niche. As my Coffee Chat with Steve & Kat partner, Katlynn Blakely-Suchomel, used to say, "Ditch the niche and take a stand for the brand." More on that in Chapter 9.

Sacred Cow #5

"You have to study and master the lessons of the greats to succeed"

This is kind of a master/apprentice concept. The thought goes that you can't possibly make it as a new freelancer until you've mastered the lessons of the legends who paved the way.

In copywriting those greats include legends like John Caples, Claude Hopkins, William Bernbach, David Ogilvy, Eugene Schwartz, and Gary Bencivenga.

A lot of copywriters spend inordinate amounts of time reading, studying, and learning about these guys. Then they tout their newfound knowledge on their websites.

"I've studied the greats like Hopkins, Ogilvy, and Schwartz, and as a result, I can help you get great results."

Seriously, I've seen this on dozens of websites, if not hundreds. Maybe they all took the same "build a copywriting website in a week" course?

The thing is, your prospects probably have no idea who these legendary copywriters are, and they don't care.

It would be like an interior designer dropping names from the pages of Architectural Digest. Nobody cares. They just want *their* house to look good.

Plus, reading and studying what these guys had to say doesn't mean you can write like them. You still have to master the skills.

Same goes for freelancing in any field. Does a new freelance photographer have to study Ansel Adams? Does a freelance designer have to study Milton Glaser?

No. It will help you have a better understanding, and you can learn a lot from them. But, again, your clients don't care. All the want to know is, *"Can you solve my problem?"* Ultimately, you have to develop your own style and brand anyway.

Why am I slaying this sacred cow? Because I see it hold back too many would-be copywriters. They stay stuck in the learning phase, which is a lot easier than going out and getting clients.

I also see it perpetuated by some legends who are still alive and now make good coin selling their programs and "bootcamps."

(Don't even get me started on that word. I can't stand it. Don't compare sitting in an air-conditioned conference room with your Starbucks and Mac Book Air and listening to speakers pitch their systems to military training.)

Are these programs and bootcamps good? Sure. Are they pricey? Usually. Do you need them to build a freelance career? Nope.

Instead of spending thousands (or tens of thousands like I have) learning a skill, go to Amazon, buy five books on your subject, read and study those, then get cracking on positioning yourself and **getting clients**. (See Chapter 10 for details on getting clients, and the Copywriter Café Facebook group for a list of recommended books.)

Mastery is an ongoing, lifetime process. Don't let a lack of mastery hold you back from making a living in your chosen freelance career.

You can make a very comfortable living at the B-level. You might as well serve clients and make money while you're on your way to A-level status, right?

Sacred Cow #6

This one is a combination of two related ideas that freelancers of all kinds hear:

"You need a big client to make it big"

and

"Aim for the big clients—that's where the money is"

"You need a big client to make it big" seemed to be the goal of a lot of my copywriting peers when I got into copywriting in 2004. The thought was: go after the Big Fish, because if you land one, you'll be set.

In other words, a big-name client would essentially "make" you. (Gangsta or Mafia-style, man!) And the fact is, it would.

The problem?

Everybody is aiming for the same Big Fish. This is terrible from a positioning standpoint. Picture this. You're standing in line with 30-40 who all want the same "job." The client sees all these hungry, hopeful freelancers groveling at their feet for a chance to get them as a client.

Chances are, they're not going to pick *any* of those who are "standing in line." Why not? Because these are mostly newer copywriters who don't have the chops yet to compete at this level.

They're going to pick the experienced pro who gets referred to them by another top copywriter, based on a track record of results. Experienced Pro copywriter isn't standing in line. He's getting Big Client to contact *him*.

See the difference?

I illustrated the futility of this "aim for big clients" method with a "stand in line" metaphor. But actually, that's a real scene I took part in myself seven times at a popular "job fair" for copywriters.

Picture this: 40 marketers in a room, set up trade show booth-style, all looking for the next hot shot copywriter to add to their team. In the same room, 350 or so copywriters who are all clamoring to get hired. Sure, it's a networking event. But you're lining up right alongside your competition, getting about 60 seconds to shake hands and swap business cards, and getting a friendly "we'll call you" as you shuffle over to the next booth.

Kind of sad, isn't it? I did pick up a good client that way. Once, in seven years. One out of about 50 or so that I aimed for, and I had a track record going in.

Don't be that freelancer waiting in line.

Who perpetuates this sacred cow that big clients are the way to go? Take a guess. The big companies who want a line of people waiting to work with them…and the companies that sponsor so-called job fairs. Don't buy into that system. The odds are stacked against you.

Big clients are great if you have the skills to get them and deliver results. But there are quicker and better ways for beginner and intermediate freelancers to break into the business, build a good base of satisfied clients, and make good money.

Employ the "hit 'em where they ain't" strategy. Go where everyone else *isn't*. It's simple supply and demand. If most freelancers are going after the big clients who pay the highest fees, take a different tack.

Go for smaller clients and more volume.

I can tell you this. Small to medium-sized businesses (SMB's) who appreciate you are much more pleasant to deal with than big clients who dictate all the terms of the working relationship, and who know they have a line of people behind you waiting for the opportunity to work with them.

If you're already a pro, go for the big clients, for sure. If you're trying to build a freelance business, hit 'em where they ain't. Don't be the freelancer standing in line.

Sacred Cow #7

We've addressed six sacred cows so far. Ideas that newcomers are presented with that are seemingly above questioning or criticism. We've talked about the myth of easy riches, the idea that you have to "pay your dues," the portfolio problem, the niche approach to building a freelance business, studying the masters, and aiming for big clients.

I have one more sacred cow to slay. I won't go into great detail here because I'm going to cover this more in Chapter 14. For now, let me state something very clearly:

There is a big difference between being a freelancer and being a business owner.

If you're a freelancer, you go from gig to gig, offering your services to anyone who's a good match. You can be a very highly-paid freelancer if you're good at what you do and keep a full schedule.

You're paid for your talents. Whether you're a freelance copywriter, graphic designer, website repair person, or content writer, your income depends entirely on *you* doing good work. You are the main attraction, as you should be.

This is the model I saw when I got into copywriting in 2004. The only model. This is the last sacred cow I want to slay for now. I was taught that...

"Being a freelancer is all about working for clients."

There's only one problem with that model.

When you stop working, your income stops, too. I can hear you asking, *"What do you mean? Isn't that how most jobs are? You stop working and you don't get paid anymore, right?"* Exactly.

While most freelancers think they've entered into some wonderful new world of limitless freedom—No boss! No more 9 to 5! No annoying co-workers! No commute!—what they've really done is bought themselves a *job*, albeit a flexible one, with themselves as the boss.

Nothing wrong with that, but make no mistake, being a highly-paid freelancer is *not* the same as building a business.

Let me give you an example. I know a number of A-level copy-writers who make a good living, somewhere between $150,000 and $300,000 a year. Good money. They've built up quite a reputation for themselves over the years, and never lack for work.

The problem is, *everything* is dependent on *them* providing the work. They're lone wolves who never built any processes or systems into their business. They never incorporated any kind of automation into the freelancing.

And no one could possibly replace them. *They* are the talent. Kind of like a popular singer or actor, with one big difference. A singer or actor is the talent, and if they stop working, sure, the new income dries up.

But chances are, that singer or actor is going to own some intellectual property. Either the publishing rights to their music (hopefully), or they'll get royalties from the movie or syndication rights.

A highly-paid freelancer (copywriter or any kind of freelancer) doesn't own any intellectual property, they don't own a business system that they can sell to someone else. They don't own a business that clients will continue coming to if they're not the featured talent. As a freelancer, they don't have any equity whatsoever.

Yes, they've been paid well over the years. But what's the point of working hard, developing a rare level of talent, and making good money, if you can't do something with it—SELL IT!—at some point?

Is copywriting (or any kind of freelance work) all about writing for clients? No. It shouldn't be!

That's the seventh sacred cow I want to slay: "Being a free-lancer is all about working for clients."

There's much more to freelancing, and that's what The Freelance Manifesto is all about.

So what's the alternative?

Build a business using copywriting skills (your copywriting skills or someone else's—it's quite easy to hire a copywriter).

Build a business you can someday SELL.

I'll go into detail on this concept in Chapter 14, "Turn Your Big Ideas and Copywriting Skills into a Profitable Venture."

In fact, I'll give you a blueprint for exactly how to do that. I'm doing it myself now, and so are lots of other Copywriter Café members.

Don't skip ahead, though. If you jump past Chapters 5-13, you'll miss the set-up and logical order that makes this entire book a **guidebook**. It's your *playbook* to *help you do freelancing different than probably 95% of freelancers out there.*

So, let me ask you. **Will you have an open mind about *building a business* versus being a freelancer?**

Yes, I know that sounds strange since I'm writing a book called *The Freelancer Manifesto*. But I have to tell you: the original title was *Death of a Freelancer*, and the subtitle was *11 Big Ideas to Overcome the Dark Side of Freelancing*.

Thankfully, I had a wonderful Skype call with author Sam Horn when I was writing this book in Quito, Ecuador. She's the author of the book, *Pop! Create the Perfect Pitch, Title, and Tagline for Anything*. She convinced me that "Death of a Freelancer" and "the dark side of freelancing" might be a little too, well…dark. On the spot, she suggested "The Freelancer Manifesto," and I'm forever in her debt. Thank you again, Sam. (Now, go buy her book, too. It's one of my favorites.)

I really was going to talk all about the DEATH of a freelancer! I know, I know…it *is* dark, and it goes against the whole gig economy thing I talked about in Chapter One.

You know what? I still AM going to talk about the death of freelancing…as we know it.

I'm coming dangerously close to giving away too much too soon, but let me end this chapter by leaving you with one thought that might cause you to question why you're even reading this book.

Freelancing is here to stay. We *are* in the gig economy. You *can* make a great living as a freelancer if you realize what you're getting into and if you do things a little differently than most freelancing. BUT…

Freelancing is NOT what you should be aiming for.

Stick with me, and I'll show you a better way.

But first, 11 things no one wants to talk about…

Chapter 5: The Dark Side of Freelancing

The Bright Side is coming, I promise!

If it seems like *The Freelancer Manifesto* has been overly dark so far, it's because I wanted you to get a clear picture of what you're getting into as a freelancer (or what you're maybe already immersed in).

The clear, unvarnished truth is that freelancing is NOT easy. **Part I is the Reality**. You probably won't make six figures your first year. You don't have to "pay your dues" for years before you make it big, but you do need a solid plan.

Before we move on, in this last chapter of Part I, I disclose 11 things no one wants to talk about.

Not just sacred cows above questioning or criticism, but topics that you won't even hear about when you're starry-eyed about the wonderful world of freelancing.

Then in Part II, The Bright Side, I'll give you **11 Big Ideas to overcome this whole dark side of freelancing, to stand out and thrive in the New Economy**.

First the problem, then the solution.

Are you with me? I assume if you've made it this far, you are.

You understand the pitfalls, and you're still on board with becoming a top-notch freelancer. And as I alluded to at the end of Chapter 4, not just a freelancer, but **the owner of a successful business**.

There's a method to my book structure here. **We start with a slow rumble and rise with a crescendo** throughout. You're especially going to like Part III, **Your Abundant Future**.

Don't skip ahead, though, or it won't have the same effect.

Ready for more revelations? Here are the 11 things no one wants to talk about:

1. You won't make six figures your first year.

Yes, I've already touched on this as the first of the sacred cows. Let me hammer the point home here.

I can count on one hand the number of freelancers I know who made six figures their first year. Out of thousands.

And you know what? Each of them has a deeper back story that they don't reveal in their "rags to riches" public story. *"I was living in my mom's basement eating Cheetos and playing video games, with $5 to my name, then I made it big through sheer determination."* Yeah, right.

They either had connections from past jobs that got them off to a super-quick start, or they had sales or marketing experience as an employee before they set out as a freelancer. Even then, it's not easy. I had 17 years of successful direct sales experience prior to freelancing, and I didn't start off with a bang.

I don't want to be discouraging. Just realistic.

Like I said, I know a handful of people who did make six figures their very first year as a freelancer. I hope you become #6! **The rest of this book is devoted to showing you how to do freelancing differently so you can**.

When you do, tell me your story! Message me at steve@-cafewriter.com and I might feature your story in my next book.

2. You won't make six figures your first year, and you *could* experience *negative* cash flow.

What!? Yes, I know people who spent more money their first year than they made.

No one talks about this because it's embarrassing. Who wants to admit their new chosen field isn't quite panning out the way they planned? Especially when you're surrounded by talk about how great freelancing is?

Quick aside here. I have to get this off my chest.

I find it extremely distasteful and unbecoming to talk about how much money you make.

I get that people are proud of their success. But why do so many freelancers, especially in the copywriting world, feel the need to announce how much money they make?

Is it to win the admiration of other freelancers? If so, why does that matter? Are they trying to sell something? Probably. Using it to gain credibility? Maybe.

There are other ways to do it. Try testimonials or case studies. No need to tell anyone how much you make.

Look, I come from a direct sales and corporate background. I understand that income is the bottom-line measure of success.

In the direct sales companies I was part of, everyone knew what everyone else's numbers were. It's part of the game. And from the sales numbers, you could pretty much figure out how much money someone made.

But in my 17 years in sales, I never once heard someone say, "I made $102,429 last year!" Very uncouth. Yet I see that all the time with freelance copywriters. Call me old fashioned, but I don't think it's kosher to talk about how much money you make. Which means, if you want to know how much money I make, you'll have to guess or do a lot of digging. Or check with WikiLeaks.

Suffice it to say, at the time of this First Edition of *The Freelancer Manifesto*, I'm doing well. My wife and I live in a nice neighborhood, we live comfortably, travel often, have two kids in college, and two more in the next two years.

I'm sure I'm above the average, but I'm not making millions. Yet.

That's all I'm going to say about money.

Back to the issue of negative cash flow...

Can you really spend more than you make your first year as a freelancer? Sure. Think about this. A lot of people start off freelancing part-time while they work a full-time job. Smart move, by the way.

When you first get into a new field, you're learning, which can cost money. If you want to get off to a quick start, you should invest in some books, programs, conferences, and coaching. A good place to start is CafeWriter.com, of course. At the very least, make sure you grab my free report there so you get the twice weekly business-building tips in your inbox.

So learning and getting set up costs money, and in the beginning, you may not be flush with client work. This is normal, but again, something no one talks about. You may very well experience negative cash flow your first year as a freelancer.

Is that any different than starting any new business? Not at all. You've probably seen the statistic that most small businesses don't make a profit in their first five years. I don't know how accurate that is, but I know a lot don't. In fact, statistics at sba.-gov show that about half of all businesses don't make it past five years. They fail.

It's a little better if you buy into a franchise, but that costs a lot of money. Franchise owners usually don't see much of a profit the first couple years either. According to a February 23, 2017, article at business.com, average annual pre-tax income for 28,500 franchisees they surveyed was $80,000. *Pre*-tax. Median pre-tax income for those franchisees was under $50,000.

That's for a franchise, with a proven system, guidance, and ongoing accountability. (All things a freelancer should have, by the way, but typically doesn't.)

Small businesses outside of a franchise system often fare worse.

So is it a big deal to experience negative cash flow your first year freelancing? No, but you don't have to.

My good friend, Alex Vermont, copywriter extraordinaire and owner of Naturally Beautiful Organics, had a good plan when he started. His rule was to not spend any money on books, programs, coaching, or events, until he made the money to pay for it from writing copy. Great rule of thumb, and I think more people should follow it.

The 11 Big Ideas in Part II will show you how to stay in the black from Day One.

3. You will have expenses you may not have thought of.

The reason it's hard to make good positive income in the beginning is because you'll have expenses. Every legitimate business does.

Guess what? If you're an employee you have it pretty good. Your employer often pays for your health insurance. You probably get a few weeks of paid vacation a year. Sick? You call in and still get paid for the day. You might even have a 401k retirement plan your employer contributes toward.

On the other hand, when you're a freelancer...

You pay for your own health insurance (if you can afford it). You provide for your own retirement. And if you want a day off, go ahead and take it, but you won't make a dime.

You'll also have normal business expense like office supplies, internet service, marketing costs, educational materials like programs and courses, coaching services, conferences, and a dozen or two other little things. The good news? All these things are tax-deductible as business expenses.

[Repeat of Legal Disclaimer: I am not an attorney or a CPA, and what follows does not constitute legal or professional advice. It's simply a way of operating that's worked well for me and others I've counseled. Please consult professional legal, financial, and tax advisers before you launch your freelance business.]

The other **good news**? You *won't* have these typical employee expenses:

a) Commuting costs

When I was in sales, I used to put 30-40,000 miles a year on my car. That's a lot of gas and wear and tear. According to the U.S. Department of Transportation, the average driver in the U.S. drives 13,476 miles a year. With gas, upkeep, and insurance, that's thousands of dollars per year, and it's not tax-deductible.

b) Time costs

Aside from the actual costs of commuting, think about the time spent driving to and from a job. Let's say you spend 30 minutes each way. One hour/day x 5 days/week x 50 weeks/year = 250 hours. That's six 40-hour work weeks in your car!

Think about what you could accomplish if you had an extra six weeks every year!

If an average freelancer makes $1,000/week, the savings from *not* having to commute is $6,000/year. That benefit *alone* makes me never want to commute again.

c) Wardrobe costs

Now, I'm not one of those people who think you should write in your pajamas just because you can. In fact, I'm adamantly opposed to it for reasons I'll write about in a minute.

On the other hand, you don't have to dress like you would if you were in a corporate or sales setting. I haven't bought a suit or been to a dry cleaners in 15 years, and while my kids would say I need to update my style a bit, I have what I'd call a comfortable, professional, affordable look.

d) Eating out costs

When I worked in the corporate world, I ate out a lot because I was on the road or needed a mental break, so I'd often grab quick meals at restaurants. That adds up. Now? I eat at home, which is cheaper and much healthier.

Yes, the benefits of freelancing far outweigh the expenses and drawbacks. I wouldn't be doing it and I wouldn't have written this book if that weren't the case.

Unlike a lot of businesses selling the freelance "dream," however, I want you to be completely aware of what you're getting into.

The fourth thing I want to address, and then put to rest…

4. You can't write in your pajamas, and you can't work at the beach.

These two ideas drive me absolutely crazy!

Why is the freelance life constantly portrayed as this lifestyle where you can either lounge around the house all day in your pajamas, or hang out at the beach with your laptop!?

Let me speak to these two issues separately. I'm not sure which lifestyle image I despise more.

First of all, the whole working in your pajamas thing (or your underwear). What's up with that? I've actually heard that phrase ("You can work in your underwear!") a number of times from people touting the freelance life.

Aside from the mental images that conjures up that are hard to erase, think about that from a practical standpoint. Even if no one sees you, can you really be productive working in your pajamas all day? (And I refuse to even acknowledge the other bad option from this point forward.)

Seriously.

I don't know *any* successful freelancer who works in their pajamas. *Not one.* To me, it's the epitome of laziness. It's like people who go out in public in their pajamas. (If you do, stop reading right now, give this book to someone with ambition and style, and don't even consider freelancing.)

I've see it once or twice—people grocery shopping or at Target in their pajamas and slippers. People tell me this is more common at Wal-Mart, but I wouldn't know anything about that.

I honestly don't know how you can focus on productive work if you're not dressed for the part. I wrote a whole blog post about this once. Weigh in at bit.ly/pajamadebate.

So let's put the pajama thing…to bed.

Even if your morning commute is 10 feet down the hallway to your home office, you'll be twice as productive (or more) if you:

- Get up at the same time every day

- Take a shower as if you're going to meet with people

- Put on some nice-looking professional clothes

- Get to your desk to do something productive first thing

Even if you're not a pajama person but usually dress pretty casual, I implore you to consider dressing well! If you're super-successful already and your standard attire is shorts, t-shirt, and sandals, well, keep it up.

But consider a wardrobe upgrade. Not formal business attire, although I think that would really ramp things up for you. But nice-looking business casual.

Do you think people like Richard Branson, Elon Musk, and Mark Zuckerberg are sitting around in t-shirts? Okay, bad example. But you and I aren't Elon and Mark. Most successful freelancers I know, especially those on their way up, are careful about the way they dress.

The other thing is, who knows when you're going to need to hop on a quick, impromptu Skype call with a client? It's more common than ever. I average two or three Skype calls a day, sometimes at the last minute with someone I'm working with. I want to look the part of a successful business person. It's part of your Personal Brand, which we'll cover a lot more in Chapter 9.

Now, the beach image…

Just like I don't know anyone who's super successful who works in their pajamas, I also don't know anyone who works at the beach.

First of all, you have to know this about me. I'm not a beach person, even when I'm not working. In April of 2010 we took a family trip to the panhandle of Florida, some of the finest white sand beaches in the world. Gorgeous.

I was bored out of my mind after one day. I mean, what do you do? Watch the waves? Play in them? Soak up the sun and relax? I tried reading a book, and couldn't do it. I wanted to sit in a normal chair and read a book like a normal person, at a coffee shop. Same thing when my wife, Emida, and I went to Oahu and the Big Island. We didn't spend five minutes at the beach.

Aside from being uninterested in beaches myself, I really don't see how anyone actually *works* at the beach. Sand and sun tan lotion aren't a good combination with laptops. And where's the desk or table? Can you really do creative, productive work from a beach chair? I don't think so.

More than the practical challenges of working the beach lifestyle, the image just doesn't work for me. "Beach bumming" is synonymous with carefree living, avoidance of work, escape from reality, and emptying your mind from thoughts of business and productive enterprise. I don't see how that equates to freelance success.

So why is the freelance lifestyle often portrayed as hanging out on the beach with a laptop? Because people want to believe it's **easy** and **fun**. It's *neither!*

Freelancing is NOT easy, and it's not fun…until you're cranking on the money. And you won't get there by hanging out on the beach.

Forget the barefoot lifestyle on the beach. Either be disciplined and sit your butt in your office chair at home, or **get yo'self to a café**! CafeWriter.com, that is. They don't call me the Café Writer for nothing! More about this in Chapter 20.

5. Others won't respect your freedom.

This is a big one.

Okay, so we've established that maybe working in your pajamas or at the beach isn't very conducive to operating a successful business. Still, you will have a serious amount of freedom.

You'll be able to establish your own hours. Want to get up early or work late at night so you can hang out with your kids during the day? That's why I chose the freelance life. I was able to attend all my kids' rehearsals, practices, lessons, and games. I was also the only dad volunteering in the classroom for five years when my kids were in elementary school.

The problem with that? People won't get that you are actually running a business. They'll think you have some fun little creative "hobby" you do from home. And they'll think you're available for all kinds of things.

Moms who are freelancers tell me they often get requests from other moms to help out with picking their kids up from school, or to host a "play date" since they're home anyway. You work from home, why not? Don't do it.

Friends who don't quite understand that working from home requires strict hours and a disciplined schedule will do the same. On a regular basis I get requests like this: *"Hey, Steve, want to grab coffee on Wednesday?"* The response I'd like to give: *"Sure. What business project are we doing to discuss, and is this going to be more beneficial for you or me?"*

I don't say that, of course.

What I do say is: *"Man, I'd love to but I'm putting in 70-hour work weeks these days, and I have some tight deadlines coming up. Maybe next month?"*

And, of course, when next month comes, same answer. I'm not saying I never have fun, and I do occasionally have a lunch or coffee appointment in the middle of the day during the week. But put parameters on your time. You have to, or people won't take what you do seriously.

Even spouses don't get it sometimes. Thankfully, Emida always has. She's been the most supportive spouse I could ask for. Even from the beginning, when I was putting in long hours and not making a ton of money, she understood.

She didn't ask me to go grocery shopping in the middle of the day, or clean the house or mow the lawn. Those things got done (usually by her), but not during normal work hours.

What about kids?

Depending on their ages, they may or may not get it either. When I started as a full-time freelance copywriter in March of 2009, my kids were 12, 10, 8, and 5. They kind of knew what I was doing, but not completely. My office was one of four bedrooms, all on the upper level.

I had to let them know I had certain "office hours," and I also had to remind them to be quiet when I had a client call. Office door closed meant I was working. Baseball hat hung on the door knob? Be quiet! On the phone.

As they got older I did away with the baseball hat thing. They knew if the door was shut, they should keep the noise level down. They also came to understand that there were payoffs to me working long and strange hours. Like being able to take off three weeks in December to go see Emida's family in Nigeria.

Or taking nine weeks in the summer to hang out as a family in Quito, Ecuador.

Yes, the freelance life has its drawbacks and **rewards**. A lot of people who have regular 8-to-5 jobs, however, won't recognize or respect your schedule.

The solution?

- Set work hours. Tell your family and friends what those hours are. Post them on your website for clients. Put parameters on your time.

- Say "no!" Don't accept every invitation for lunch or coffee just because you can. Set a precedent early on and be disciplined with your time.

- Get your family on board. Let them know you'll be putting in some long hours, and tell them what your office hours are. Then stick to them as much as possible.

- Don't answer the phone during work hours. From anyone, including clients or prospects, unless it's a scheduled call. I'll explain this later.

- Same thing with the doorbell. Don't answer the door for anyone. I get packages from Amazon all the time but I let the UPS or FedEx person leave it on the front porch.

- Hide from people! Make it very hard for people to reach you.

- Even if no one else puts demands on your time, be disciplined yourself. Don't run errands during the day. Don't get lazy and do outside activities like cleaning the house or mowing the lawn with the excuse that you need a "mental break." Set office hours and stick to them.

- Speaking of, consider hiring someone to clean your house and mow your lawn. Before I was married, when I was in sales, I had a housekeeper and a lawn guy. Now, Emida enjoys doing outside work, so we don't hire anyone. No one likes cleaning, but that's what kids are for, right? Bottom line: I don't do anything I can get someone else to do

- Last thing—set rewards for yourself, especially if you have family involved. If your spouse or kids have to put up with you and your odd freelance schedule, make sure they're the beneficiaries of the work and discipline, too.

In our house, trips have always been the big reward. In addition to the international travel I mentioned, over the years I've also taken Emida on a number of trips, including places like Buenos Aires, Paris, and numerous trips to New York.

Also, as they were growing up, each of my four kids got a one-on-one trip with me when they were 6, 9, 12, and 15 years old. So, yes, Emida let me go on 15 different one-on-one trips with my kids so far while she held down the fort at home! We traipsed off to New York, Los Angeles, Toronto, Chicago, Boston, D.C., and even Iceland and Greenland. Those were some of the best memories I ever had (and I hope Alex, Solomon, Sapphina, and Zaria can say the same). I have one more to go, with Zaria, in 2018. Any recommendations? Let me know.

Whatever your system is, make sure you set up something to reward yourself and your family, and do it at every step of the way. You don't have to wait until you're making the big bucks. I didn't.

Still with me? Again, **we're going to get to The Bright Side in Part II**, but I want you to be aware of the Dark Side—Reality—first. Not to scare you off, but so you know what you're in for.

I can tell you this. I wouldn't trade the freelance lifestyle for anything.

Good thing, because even if I wanted to, I don't think I could go back to being an employee. And I'm not sure anyone would hire me. I'm 50 years old, I haven't had a resume or interviewed for a job since 2001, and I don't do well in corporate cubicles. I've been working for myself for so long, I'm afraid I'd make a terrible employee. Too stifling, among many other things.

Now, while you and I have a positive view of freelancing, I need to let you in on a little secret…

6. "Freelancer" sounds like you can't get a job.

Ha! It's something to be aware of. To any future employers (if you ever plan to go back to looking for a job), "freelancer" implies that you were between jobs a little too long, or that you tried to do your own thing and it didn't work out.

I would not recommend ever putting "freelance" anything on your resume.

You might not care what family, friends, or unknown future bosses might think of the word "freelancer." But how about clients? From what I've seen and heard from clients, it's a very subtle thing.

Here's my take on it. Call yourself a "freelancer," and some clients might think:

"She's just flitting about from job to job. She'll probably be happy to get work from me, and as such, I'll be able to dictate the terms. I also know freelancers have virtually no overhead, since they're not operating a real business, so I probably don't need to pay her the same rate I'd pay an agency."

"Freelancer" has connotations of loose, carefree, catering to clients versus being in charge, lack of business systems, flexible payment terms, and flexible arrangements overall.

Not so good if you are the freelancer. See where that image of a freelancer might hurt you? It's not that a client is going to consciously take advantage of you if that's how they think of freelancers, although they might.

It's more about how the overall positioning in the client-service provider relationship gets skewed a bit.

A client who's hiring a freelancer they think is hungry for the work is going to think they have the upper hand. They'll be calling the shots and dictating the terms of the project.

On the other hand, if you promote yourself as a *business owner* **who has a solution to their problem**, and *you* are qualifying *them* to see if they're a good fit for what you do, then *you* are in control. See the difference?

The positioning between you and prospective clients evens out. You'll have an easier time attracting business. They'll have more respect for you from the start, and you won't get as many questions about your fees or terms. More on this in Chapter 9, "Build Your Personal Brand," and Chapter 17, "Why I'm Burying 'Freelancer' for Good."

For now, realize that calling yourself a freelancer may not be your best play.

Next, I touched on this briefly at the end of Chapter 1, "The Gig Economy is Here to Stay"…

7. Supply and demand favor the client over the freelancer.

It's simple economics. I don't care what anybody tells you. No matter what type of freelancer you are—copywriter, graphic designer, social media manager—there are more of *you* than there are good *clients*.

"Wait a second, Steve," I can hear you saying. *"How do you know that for a fact? You don't even know what my area of specialty is. I've found a hidden, in-demand niche that other freelancers don't even know about yet."*

Fair enough. I say enjoy your secret, non-competitive niche now, because it's not going to last.

(And quickly grab a copy of one of my other books, *47 Ways to Do Copywriting: Fresh new ways to position yourself and create a profitable business*, available to Café Writer members now and at Amazon soon.)

How do I know it won't last? Because you can't operate a business without being seen, especially online. Some other freelancer somewhere on Earth is going to find you. And if they realize you're in an unknown niche overflowing with hungry clients, guess what? They're going to jump in!

Pretty easy to do, right? There's a pretty low barrier to entry to become a freelancer of any kind these days. Yes, you need some skills. But you don't need any specialized training, education, or certification. Want to be a freelance copywriter? Soak up some great free information online, and voilà! You're a copywriter. Want to specialize in a hot, new, obscure niche? That won't take long either.

My point is this. Supply of freelancers always exceeds the demand. Or it will soon. Nature abhors a vacuum, as they say. And if there's a gap in the marketplace, it will soon get filled.

Does this mean there's no hope or a freelancer to make it big? Is freelancing a futile proposition? Am I writing this book in vain!?

Not at all.

Then, what do you have to do?

- Differentiate (Chapter 6)

- Get creative (Chapter 7)

- Build your Personal Brand (Chapter 9)

- Stake your claim (Chapter 10)

- Get better at marketing and selling than your competition (Chapter 11)

- Scale your business (Chapter 15)

That last one might be the most important.

Go beyond a freelance operation that is mostly dependent on you and your skills. Ignore the law of supply and demand at your peril. *Acknowledge the law and play by its rules and you will emerge the victor.* Yes, even in a sea of freelancers.

8. "Follow the follower" is another dangerous place to be.

Here's what I mean. In my last point about supply and demand, I mentioned that when there's a gap in the marketplace, it gets filled.

For example, let's say a new technology emerges on the scene, like drones a few years ago. It's a burgeoning market, and a number of new companies manufacturing drones emerge on the scene.

Some enterprising young freelance copywriter decides he's going to specialize in helping drone companies bring their product to the masses with a proprietary direct response marketing system.

That's great, and he probably has the market to himself for a while. A few problems, though.

First, unless he scales his business fast, there's no way he can serve all the new drone companies. Second, since he can't serve them all, other observant, ambitious copywriters will soon move in and fill that demand. That's great, too, up to the point where supply = demand.

The third problem is that freelancers of all kinds tend to play "follow the follower." They watch what other freelancers are doing, look for attractive opportunities, and follow suit.

Result? You end up with a lot of look-alike freelancers who've been following the followers.

A better approach? **Think ahead of the curve** (the first topic in Part II, The Bright Side). Also, stay under the radar as much as you can when you do come up with a Big Idea (Chapter 8). And for about the tenth time so far in this book, and something I'll keep pounding home—build your Personal Brand! Only *you* can do *you*. More on that in Chapter 9.

One more thing about playing "follow the follower." Be careful of buying and following the latest "Six Figures in Six Months"-type program for freelancers.

- If it sounds too good to be true, it might be. Exaggerated claims sell programs, but they often don't pan out.

- "Cookie cutter" programs are great for franchisees and network marketers. Not so great for freelancers trying to distinguish themselves. "One-size-fits-all" usually doesn't.

- If *you* are buying the program, chances are so are hundreds of other freelancers. The gap that may have existed when the program's author wrote the program will quickly be gone when that many new suppliers (freelancers) flood the market with their look-alike services.

The law of supply and demand is always in effect.

A better solution to playing "follow the follower"? Think ahead of the curve (Chapter 6) and when you find a gap in the marketplace, keep it to yourself! Stay under the radar (Chapter 8).

Now, here I am telling you to be careful of buying programs that promise easy, how-to, freelance riches. Yet I'm in the business of promoting my own programs. What's the difference? I believe in systems and processes, for sure.

Beyond that? You should develop your own Personal Brand and you should get *someone* (me or another coach) to work with you one-on-one and give you feedback and guidance specifically tailored to your situation.

At the very least, join a membership site where you'll get training, resources, feedback, advice, and ideas. There are dozens out there, and I'm a little biased, but I think Café Writer is one of the best. The low monthly cost for a Premier Membership is a no-brainer investment if you're a writer or copywriter.

Bottom line: Don't play "follow the follower." **Stand out and be an original**. Let me know if I can help you in any way at

steve@cafewriter.com.

Three more Dark Side issues before we cross over to the Light…

9. Making *really* good money is a long shot.

Thanks for hanging with me. One of the reasons I've spent this much time spelling out the challenges of freelancing is because *no one else is!* They're all sugar-coating it to sell the dream.

The carefree, living large, barefoot-on-the-beach-with-your-laptop freelance lifestyle is a delusion.

Treat your freelancing like a business, as though you've put up $100-200K like you would to start many small businesses or franchises. Then listen to the suggestions in this book, and you'll have a much better chance of success.

Speaking of your odds of success…what are they? Depends on how you define success.

I'm a huge baseball fan, and hopefully you have some familiarity with the game so you can understand my analogy. But first, I think anyone who is getting established as a freelancer today, getting clients, and earning enough to pay their bills, is a success. If that's you, I applaud you.

I'm also guessing you wouldn't be freelancing if you didn't want to make some *good* money. I'm assuming you want to make *the major leagues.* Now, keep in mind, I have no idea what actual income numbers are for freelancers. It's next to impossible to tell. It's not something the government tracks, like the Department of Labor statistics on employee salaries for various professions.

Freelancing is a big ol' Wild West free-for-all, and there's no way to pin down numbers. Think of all the freelancers out there in the world. And for now, just think of *your* area. If you're a website designer, think of all the website designers out there. If you're a graphic designer, think of all the graphic designers.

Since I'm a copywriter, I'm going to use this example. All the copywriters out there are like all the baseball players in the country who dream of playing beyond high school or Babe Ruth League ball. Guys that want to play in college or the minor leagues and aspire to hit the big-time, Major League Baseball.

In fact, there are 486,537 high school baseball players in the U.S. There are 56,578 college baseball players, 5,856 minor league players, and 750 Major League players. Not great odds, right?

A quick Google search and a little bit of research shows as many freelance copywriters as high school baseball players! Insane competition (but don't worry, **I'll show you how to bypass 95% of it in this book**).

If you're making up to $100,000 a year, you're probably with about 90% of your peers. You're playing high school ball or maybe in the minor leagues. That's not to demean your skills, your hustle, or your income. You're in the game, and you're making some money! Congratulations.

When you get to $100,000 and maybe up to $200,000, you're doing really well. Making good money, and you've got a pretty good shot at going further and making the Major League. I'd call this Triple A ball. In baseball, a lot of guys at the Triple A level get called up to the Major League team.

You have very solid skills, you're making a name for yourself and getting noticed, and if you keep practicing fundamentals, get some good coaching, and sharpen your game, you could be playing in the Major League. Triple A players/freelancers are in the top 5%.

Now, get up into the $200,000 to $500,000 range, and you're there. You're in the Major League, top 1%, and pretty much set for life.

Are these your odds of getting to these numbers? I don't know exactly, but I bet the baseball and copywriter numbers are close to each other.

My point?

Making it to the "Major League" of copywriting or any freelance specialty is NOT easy. It's a long shot to make the really good money.

If you're content playing in the minor leagues (and you can make good money there), you still have to work hard and do things right. The good news? **The higher you go, the less competition there is**.

There's a TON of competition at the minor league levels. Set your sights higher, and do the things it takes to rise up the ranks, and it gets easier. I call it the Major League Paradox.

If I could give you one piece of advice here, it's this: Aim for the Major League. Decide that you're in this for the long haul, and do the things necessary to out-hit, out-run, and out-slug your competition (to keep the baseball analogy going).

Hmm…that gives me an idea for a tagline:

Outwit, Outlast, Outplay.

Sounds familiar. It might already be taken.

How about Out-think, Out-work, Out-promote? We might have something there.

Two more things no one wants to talk about…

10. Not having a boss is not good!

One of the biggest reasons people decide to quit their jobs and become a freelancer? They don't like their boss. He's too demanding. He knows less than you do. He's lazy. He doesn't value your contributions to the company. He doesn't give you enough time off…and on and on.

It's human nature not to like your boss, right? Tell me you never had this experience. While you're working at a job you don't like, for a boss you really don't like, you start to fantasize:

"It would be so great to work for myself."

"I can't wait for the day when I can quit and start my own business."

"They're going to miss me when I'm gone."

"I'll be moving on to better things and he'll probably be stuck at this job forever."

"I am so much better than this. I deserve better."

Or simply, *"This job sucks."*

I'm telling you, I've talked to (and later counseled) hundreds of freelancers. It's amazing how many of them seemed like they were running *away* from something (a job or boss they didn't like) *more than* they were running *toward* something.

Either way, whether you get into freelancing after leaving a job you like or don't like, I'll let you in on something you never hear freelancers admit:

Having a boss is a good thing!

"What!? You're a successful freelance copywriter. How can you say having a boss is good? Sacrilege!"

Yes, I've actually gotten that reaction from people who think I'm dis-owning the noble calling of being a freelancer by saying bosses are good.

Here's what I mean. There's a reason for the managerial structure you see in the corporate world. It works.

Managers and "bosses" are vital for the efficiency and profitability of a company. Bosses:

- Get more out of you than you would operating on your own.

- Keep you on track with feedback and performance reviews.

- Give you goals to aim for.

- Play an important role in between management and employee-level positions.

Bottom line: a boss will get more production out of you than you will get operating on your own.

And *that's* what's missing in the freelance world! We don't have anyone keeping us accountable or on track. No one who sits down with us for an annual or quarterly performance review. **No one who's expecting big things from us**.

I'll say it again: **Not having a boss is not a good thing**.

Now, if you're an extremely disciplined person, you set high goals for yourself and always achieve them, and don't need anyone to hold your feet to the fire, I applaud you.

You're one of the rare ones, and you'll have no trouble succeeding as a freelancer.

But if you're anything like me, when you have no one watching what you're doing and keeping you accountable, you might occasionally get a bit lazy.

You might not get as much done every week as you would with a boss, or a "sales manager," watching your numbers.

If that describes you, you're not alone. I'd say most of the population in any line of work needs a "boss" of some kind. Even freelancers. *Especially* the freelancers, because you know what happens if you don't? You simply won't reach your full potential as a freelancer.

"I became a freelancer in part to be my own boss. Now you're telling me I need a boss!?"

Well, not a boss per se. A coach. And if this sounds completely self-serving because I am a business coach for freelancers, you got me. Yes, this is partly a plug for my services. I work with freelance writers and copywriters who are trying to build a business.

I do one-time coaching calls, ongoing monthly calls, and small group business immersion retreats. **See Services at CafeWriter.com for details**.

I can't work with everyone reading this who needs a coach, so I advise you to seek out a coach. If I'm booked solid**, I can give you recommendations.** Email me at steve@cafewriter.com.

If all those options are out of your budget at this time, at the very least, join a free community like my Copywriter Café Facebook group to help keep you on track. A group like this gives you ideas, advice, encouragement, feedback, and if you ask for it, accountability.

One last option I highly recommend that's super affordable. Join a membership site like Café Writer. Mine provides a lively (private) discussion forum, copy critiques, feedback on ideas, business-building advice, and ongoing training and resources.

It's not a substitute for having a coach, but at only $25/month, it's the next best thing. Check it out at CafeWriter.com.

Finally, the last thing no one in the freelance world likes to talk about...

11. Working for other people is NOT where the big money is.

I'll explain…

Offering your freelance writing, photography, graphic design, copywriting, or website-building services to other people is fine.

It's what most freelancers do. You have a skill, you hang out your virtual shingle offering that skill, and people hire you. Pretty straightforward, right?

But what happens when someone in your own profession hires you to do the same work that they can do themselves? And probably do better?

Let's say you're a freelance copywriter. You have solid skills, you've had a few good clients, and you're starting to make a name for yourself, little by little. Through some connections and hustle, you get the attention of an A-level copywriter who is known by everyone. This person has made millions as a copywriter and is miles ahead of you talent-wise.

Yet Mr. A-level copywriter hires *you* to write some copy for *him*.

This actually happened to me twice, and at first I couldn't figure it out. I was thrilled to get the work, and I got paid quite well. I wondered *why* they hired me, though.

Both of these guys were much better copywriters than I was. They could write a much better promotion than me. My biggest thought was, *"Why don't they write the copy themselves?"*

Then it dawned on me. Yes, they were better copywriters than I was. But their time was much better spent *working on their business* than on doing one small part of that business, the copywriting.

This is the lesson I want to pound home in this last point of Part I, Reality:

Your time is better spent building your own business than offering the one service that other people will hire you for.

I don't care if you're a copywriter or a photographer or any other kind of freelancer.

No matter what type of freelancer you are, you will always come out ahead in the long run if you work on building your business more than you work on the one skill that you specialize in.

In my case, working with the two A-level copywriters, I looked in-depth at what they were doing. **I studied each of their business models and became determined to follow their lead**.

One of them, Mark Everett Johnson, was part-owner at the time of a publishing business, American Lantern Press. This quiet, under-the-radar business was generating huge revenue every year. I don't have exact numbers, but well into the millions, for a business with relatively little overhead or employee costs.

They had gotten in early on the preparedness niche, also known as the "prepper" niche. They provided valuable information in the form of books, guides, programs, and a monthly *print* newsletter (something I'm a big fan of and will be talking about a lot more in this book and at cafewriter.com).

American Lantern Press grew by doing a few things very well. They:

- Identified a narrow target audience.

- Provided that audience with valuable information packaged in a way they couldn't get elsewhere.

- Established their "value ladder" early on. In other words, they had a progression of information their audience wanted, from free to mid-range and high-range products.

- Built large email *and* direct mail lists.

- Engaged their audience on a regular basis.

- Built systems and processes into everything they did.

- **Took themselves out of the equation**.

This last one is key if you're going to build a business rather than be a freelancer-for-hire. At some point on your freelance path, if you really want to grow a business and get big, you have to relinquish parts of the business. You have to realize that the tasks, the fulfillment of services, are really just one part of your business.

For example, if you're a wedding photographer who's really good at your craft, there are only so many weddings you can shoot. You can only be in one place at a time. If you're thinking big, however, here's what you could do:

Instead of being Jane Smith, wedding photographer, you could call your business Lasting Memories or something like that. Hire two freelance photographers to start with.

You concentrate on bringing in new business, let them do all the wedding photo shoots and pay them maybe 50% of what you're charging.

At the same time, you start growing your email list. You take a different approach than most wedding photographers, however. Instead of advertising the actual wedding photography services, you take a bigger, holistic approach. You hire a freelance copywriter to write a special report called, "The Three Things Every Bride Should Stop Wasting Money On." You put this as a free download on your website in exchange for someone's email address.

Lots of ways to drive traffic to your website, and I'm not going to go into all of them here because marketing methods change by the week these days. You could drive traffic to your website using Facebook ads, affiliate marketing, social media campaigns, or even direct mail. Yes, even Google and Amazon use direct mail in 2017 to promote their services, and they OWN the internet! So any number of ways you can get people to your website and grab your special report.

From there, you continue email marketing to them, giving the bride valuable tips for her upcoming big day (and many brides start looking ahead a year or two in advance). You're giving value before you try to get a customer.

You're doing things different than the typical wedding photographer. You're thinking long-term, not just snagging a client for one photo shoot.

Along with the email messages providing useful information, you're weaving in your services in a natural way. It feels natural, not forced, and positions you as an authority on wedding photography, not someone who's just trying to get their business.

It wouldn't take long using this style of marketing to get booked up solid.

Then, what do most wedding photographers do once the wedding is over? They thank the client, maybe ask for referrals, and move on.

Not you.

You're not a freelance *photographer*, you're a *business owner* who's creating a *mini-empire* based on your expertise. Instead of simply trading your time for dollars you're looking at the big picture and running your business.

So you have an email list and a direct mail list. Once the wedding is over you start promoting the idea of creating lifetime memories at every stage—early married life, babies, young children. You send the client special offers mixed in with your normal monthly newsletter and emails. You become a trusted source as their family photographer, and they come back to you again and again. You're in the lifetime memories business, not the wedding photography business.

See the difference? That's just one example I came up with on the spot as I was writing this chapter. I have no doubt it will work even though I'm not basing it on any real wedding photography business I've ever seen.

I know, because it's employing principles of **direct response marketing**, which works for all kinds of businesses everywhere. *This* is what I help freelancers do. I help freelancers go from the gig-to-gig scenario to building a true business.

Now do you see why Mr. A-level copywriter hired me, an up-and-coming copywriter who was good but not nearly at his level? His time was better spent running his business rather than completing one task, the copywriting.

By the way, I was paid quite well for my work. I also know that the promotion I wrote generated a lot of money for them, so it was a good return on investment.

Real quick, let me tell you about the other situation where a top copywriter hired me. Dan Kennedy had a client who was paying him six figures to work on a big campaign. Dan needed junior copywriters to do some background research and provide bits and pieces of copy. Sure, he could have done it himself, but his time was much better spent handling the client and coming up with big strategy ideas than the minutiae of research and copywriting.

I won't go into detail here, but all you have to do is Google "Dan S. Kennedy" and look him up on Amazon to see what an incredibly successful business he's created. Early on he could have easily made $150,000 to $250,000 a year being a freelance copywriter. He chose to take the bigger-picture view of building a business and now he's probably worth 100 times those amounts.

I'll say it one more time, being a freelancer for other people is *not* where the big money is. **Building and operating your own business is the place to be**.

In Part I, I've given you the **Reality** of freelancing in today's world. I've given you a little bit of the good, but mostly the bad and the ugly. **Don't worry, the good part is coming next!** I didn't hold back. I'm not here to sugarcoat the freelance lifestyle.

The fact is, it's not for everyone. And even if it's for you, (I assume it is if you're still reading), it's not about only working a few hours a day. It's not about working barefoot at the beach. It's not about tapping away on your keyboard writing about your passion.

It's about using your skills to fill a demand in the marketplace, position yourself as the best solution, and build a true business by creating a structure and systems that can eventually run smoothly with or without you.

I've described the Gig Economy, and hopefully shown you how you can fit into it. I've told you my story, which should give you confidence that you can be successful, too. You've had a chance to see what your Freelance Quotient™ is. (Go to freelancequiz.com.)

I've laid out and slayed the seven sacred cows of freelancing— seven ideas that aren't necessarily true, but nobody ever seems to question. And I've described 11 things no one wants to even talk about.

So far, I've given you the cold, unvarnished truth. And you know what? It's going to ruffle a few feathers. The people and organizations whose ideas I've called out aren't going to like it. So be it.

For a long time, I held back on writing this book out of fear. Fear that the people I was calling out wouldn't like me anymore. Fear that I'd get blackballed in the copywriting industry. Fear that I might be wrong.

I remember telling a friend, "Maybe I should hold back, keep my opinions to myself, and just focus on building my own freelance copywriting business." After all, from my second year on, since 2010, my business was humming along quite nicely. I have no doubt that if I had focused completely on writing for clients you would know me as a top A-level copywriter, and I'd be making a great living only as a freelance copywriter.

But the more I investigated the whole freelance lifestyle and pulled back the curtain on some of the dirty little secrets of the industry, the more I knew I had to get the word out. I felt a duty, an obligation, to expose the light on the Dark Side of Freelancing.

I've been on the inside for a dozen years now, and you know what? I'm no longer afraid.

I really don't care if some people don't like me. There's no way an entire industry could blackball me to the point where I couldn't get work. It's a big ol' world out there and 98% of my audience has never heard of the people, organizations, and ideas that I'm calling out anyway.

The other thing is, I'm no longer afraid that I might be wrong about these ideas. I've seen them and lived them myself. More than that, I've talked with thousands of freelancers over the past five years and verified these ideas.

I've sat down face-to-face with hundreds of freelancers and heard their stories. My exclusive membership site for freelance writers gives me daily insights and inside information on the real deal for freelancers. And my Facebook group of over 6,000 members gives me even deeper perspective on the day-to-day life of freelancers.

I see the challenges and obstacles, and I also know what the solutions are. In Part II, The Bright Side, I give you 11 big ideas to overcome the Dark Side of Freelancing. These 11 Big Ideas are the result of tens of thousands of observations of freelancers, thousands of online conversations I've had with freelancers, hundreds of one-on-one coaching sessions, and about 20 multi-day retreats and seminars that I've hosted, attended by about 200 freelancers.

Now that you've seen the truth and gotten a good picture of the **reality** of freelancing, are you ready for The Bright Side?

I wouldn't have written this book if I didn't believe from the bottom of my heart and depths of my soul that freelancing and its natural extension, **building a business**, offers the most rewarding professional experience you can imagine. Come along with me as we cross over to the other side.

Part II: The Bright Side: 11 Big Ideas to Overcome The Dark Side of Freelancing

Congratulations! You made it through The Dark Side.

I lingered there for a while for a few reasons. I didn't want to gloss over the negative aspects of freelancing. There are plenty, as you can see. Better to know up front what you're getting into, right?

And if you're already firmly entrenched as a freelancer but only caught glimpses of The Dark Side up until now? No time like the present to confront reality.

The other reason we delved deep into The Dark Side? I wanted to scare some people off. We have enough competition the way it is! Why encourage more?

Besides, freelancers who dance around the edges, never truly committing, are doing themselves and potential clients a disservice. Clients who unwittingly hire them get subpar results. And the uncommitted freelancer prolongs the inevitable—a return to employee status (which can often be the best thing to do).

So, welcome to Part II, The Bright Side.

In this section I'm going to give you 11 Big Ideas to overcome The Dark Side of Freelancing, and to stand out and thrive in the New Economy.

Now that you know the 11 things no one wants to talk about, you can move on. Forget about those and focus on the 11 Big Ideas. These are ideas fleshed out over my own successful freelancing path since 2004. They're a result of thousands of hours of counseling and coaching freelance copywriters from 2011 to the present.

And, they're ideas I developed as I planned, prepared for, and hosted 10 business immersion retreats since 2013, including the Northwoods Plunge™, the Big Ideas Retreat™, and what I used to call the Ultimate Writing Retreat™. By the way, as of the publication date of this book, I'm the only copywriter hosting intimate multi-day events like this. We focus on helping you build a business using your copywriting skills. Check out cafewriter.com for more information.

These are also *timeless principles*, not hot marketing tips of the moment. These principles will be as relevant in five years as they are today. Any one of the 11 Big Ideas put into action will give you and your business a slight edge. Implement a *few* of them or *all* of them over time and you'll be *untouchable*. Ready? Let's rock and roll.

Chapter 6: Think Ahead of the Curve

If you've never considered yourself a trendsetter, now would be the time to start.

In the last chapter I pointed out 11 things no one wants to talk about. Number eight was "Follow the follower" is a dangerous place to be.

You see this with all kinds of freelancers. Someone will have a good idea and get into a new niche, or often a new service. These are the risk-takers, the leaders, the trailblazers. They're not waiting for something tried and tested. They're **thinking ahead of the curve** and coming up with the new ideas to make a name for themselves and break away from the pack.

What happens once they do come up with a great idea? Fools rush in. Okay, that's harsh.

Not necessarily *fools*, but look-alikes, copy cats, and wanna-bes. It's human nature and it's the nature of business. Nothing you can do to stop it.

And that's okay because if *you* are the one thinking ahead of the curve, you'll usually have an advantage over the freelancers coming late to the table.

A few years ago, fintech was a hot new thing (financial technology, including any technological innovations having to do with financial literacy and education, retail banking, investments, and crypto-currencies like Bitcoin). I know a number of copywriters who got in early and established themselves as specialists serving the fintech market.

They were able to establish themselves early, make a lot of good contacts, and basically write their own ticket. Now? Google "fintech copywriters" and you get 111,000+ results. At least that's what came up for me in June of 2017. And the first one was a "badass" fintech copywriter! Those are two terms that don't seem to go together.

It also speaks to my Sacred Cow #4. This is the problem when you focus on a niche rather than a service and developing your own brand. Hard to distinguish yourself, easy for others to copy.

One more example. Most graphic designers kind of look alike, sound alike, and offer the same services. Doing research for this book, I looked at dozens and dozens of graphic designer websites, and they all looked remarkably similar, with the same services. Hmm…kind of like copywriters' websites.

But then I stumbled upon lemonly.com. Wow! Refreshing look and feel, and they bill themselves as an "Infographic Design Agency," which is pretty cool. They also specialize in "visual storytelling," a term I didn't see on any other graphic design website.

I don't know if Lemonly was the first to do this, but they came up high in the search engine results when I looked for "info-graphic designer."

There are lots of designers offering that service now, but this was the agency I'd call if I needed anything like that.

My point is, you *have to* stand out somehow, and the one of the best ways to do that is to think ahead of the curve.

Can you make good money as a follower? Yes, as long as you develop your own Personal Brand (see Chapter Nine).

Whether you're first into a new space or 51st, you have to do *something* to stand out. And even if you are later coming into a new market, there are ways to analyze your competition and position yourself against them. We'll talk about that more in Chapter Nine, too.

Your best bet, though, is to **think ahead of the curve**, and **come up with original ideas** instead of copying others.

So, how do you come up with these ideas? I found three ways to be very effective:

Read, think, and talk to intelligent people!

1. Read

Read the *New York Times* and the *Wall Street Journal,* and your local paper (if you have local clients). Read classic literature like Hemingway and Hugo, as well as airport paperbacks by John Grisham and Stephen King.

Read magazines. Legendary copywriter Eugene Schwartz (author of *Breakthrough Advertising,* a book every copywriter and marketer should read) told copywriters they should read magazines like People, Vanity Fair, and even the National Enquirer, to understand their audience and be able to better write to them.

I subscribe to about a dozen magazines, including Wired, Fast Company, Entrepreneur, Fortune, People (I'm listening to Schwartz), Robb Report (excellent for getting you thinking BIG), Inc., Entertainment Weekly, Forbes, and a few others. I read a couple dozen more at my health club while I'm doing my daily executive workout (sitting in the sauna).

Read! And keep a notebook with you when you do. I even write in the sauna with my Rite in the Rain® notebooks and pens. Yeah, people think I'm weird. We writers are, kind of.

(And I do plan to use my saunawriter.com domain name at some point. No pictures, though.)

2. Think!

You simply have to spend time deep thinking about Big Ideas. The reading with a pen and a notebook thing helps with this. Lots more in the next chapter. Then...

3. Talk to interesting people.

If you're reading and thinking a lot, you'll have lots of interesting things to talk about with interesting people. Boring people talk about the weather and sports. Not you (or me)!

People like us who think ahead of the curve talk about **ideas**.

When I'm in my office, I spend two or three hours a day talking with copywriters who are trying to build their businesses. I ask questions to get them thinking in a different way. I challenge them. I offer critiques if they ask. We engage in interesting discussions about offbeat ideas.

My copywriting clients have businesses as diverse as fitness studios, accounting practices, publishing companies, investment firms, and vacation rental homes. Interesting discussions arise in every conversation with clients, and these often get me thinking of new business angles, for them and for myself.

If it's not copywriters or clients, or my wife and kids (quite intelligent, all of them), I'm pretty selective about how I spend my time and with whom. The more you hang out with interesting, intelligent people, the more you'll also be coming up with ideas to stay ahead of the curve. It's a general principle, and somewhat abstract, but a foundational principle that the other 10 Big Ideas depend on.

Think ahead of the curve by coming up with original ideas, test them on a small scale to see if they work, and then go all out. Go all out promoting yourself to your audience while keeping as quiet as can be to your competition (details in Chapter Eight).

Do this and you won't have to worry about stomping out your competition. You'll only see them at a distance in your rearview mirror.

Let's dive deeper into this idea thing...

Chapter 7: Become an Idea Generator

People don't think. We've become a culture of idea *consumers.*

Idea consumers and brainless, mind-numbed, device-addicted robots.

Look around. No matter where you go people's heads are buried in their smartphones and tablets. Constantly.

Seriously, you can't go anywhere, at least in the States, without seeing almost everyone immersed in the excitement of checking Facebook or their text messages. *Consuming* other people's information.

I say consuming, because no one is producing written content on a smartphone. Video, yes, but not written content.

Nobody communicates anymore. Go out to eat and observe. Entire tables of people spending good money on nice food and ambience, and what do they do as soon as the dishes are cleared? Whip out their smartphones. God forbid they should have to talk to each other. The art of conversation is dying.

People don't think. They don't know how to communicate with each other. And they're getting dumber.

This was made glaringly obvious to me when I removed myself from the zombie phone culture of the States. For 10 weeks at the beginning of 2016 I hung out in Quito, Ecuador. That's where I wrote this book, which is one of the main reasons I went.

As a writer I'm always observing people. I find it fascinating to watch, listen, and learn. I had been to Ecuador before for a total of 13 weeks. Back again for ten weeks in 2016, I expected Ecuadorians to have caught up with North Americans with smartphone usage. I was partly right. They had phones all right, and tablets. They just don't check them incessantly.

People carry them, but I almost *never* saw anyone check their device, especially when they were in a group of people. Never.

You know what they did? They talked to each other!

And you know what else I never saw? Not once? I never saw someone in a coffee shop with a laptop.

Again, people go to cafes. But get this—it's super radical—they go there to drink coffee and talk to each other!

None of the cyber squatters you see in Starbucks all over the U.S., camped out with their backpack and MacBook Pro, milking their tall coffee for four hours. (And, to answer your mental thought, no I didn't camp out with my laptop. I wrote this entire book long-hand, one coffee at a time, one hour at a time. Finish the coffee, go to another café, or go home and write some more. No cyber squatting for me. End of rant.)

What does this long prelude have to do with you as a freelancer?

Well, just like people in general don't *think* anymore, and have lost the fine art of communication, *so have freelancers*, which means if you can become known as an Idea Generator you will stand out big-time in your field. You will quickly rise above the competition.

Now, you would think freelance creative types like writers, copywriters, and designers, would be an endless supply of fresh new ideas.

Not so. You'd be amazed at how even freelance writers have a hard time coming up with ideas.

Let me back up here for a minute. When I say you should be an Idea Generator, I mean on two levels.

1. You need to brainstorm and generate ideas for *yourself.*

For your own marketing efforts, your Personal Brand, and your business development.

Unless you want to be a look-alike, copycat freelancer who follows the trends, you need to generate Big Ideas for yourself to stay ahead of the curve as we discussed in the last chapter.

We are in a competitive business. Ideas get you noticed. Ideas create leaders that others want to follow (and buy from). Ideas are currency. Ideas build businesses. Be an Idea Generator!

2. You need to brainstorm and generate ideas for your *clients* and *customers.*

See, it's a whole lot easier to be what I call an "order taker" than to be an Idea Generator. Order takers offer a service, say photography, website design, copywriting, or logo design.

It's easy to hang out your virtual shingle as an order taker because the barrier to entry is extremely low. Read a few books, buy a camera, fancy yourself a camera buff, take a class, and voilà! You're a photographer. If someone comes to you and says, "My daughter needs senior pictures done, can you do that?" The answer of course is, "Yes." You take the order, provide the service, collect the payment, and move on.

Same thing with a freelance copywriter. You advertise that you write great landing pages. The client calls you up, tells you exactly what they're trying to sell, asks if you can write it, and you answer, "Yes."

Sure, both scenarios will involve a client consultation. At a basic level, both clients can be served effectively by listening, asking a few clarifying questions, and delivering exactly what they want. Order takers.

When I was in direct sales from 1986 to 2003, we called lower-level salespeople "order-takers." They may have been working hard, calling on prospects, offering their services, but they weren't doing anything to create sales. They were essentially working hard enough that every once in a while they'd stumble upon someone who really wanted what they were selling (a "lay down" in sales parlance), and they'd "take their order."

Now, picture the more lucrative way of operating. The experienced professional salesperson calls on the same prospects. But instead of simply offering his services, he's planting seeds of ideas with his prospects. Asking thought-provoking questions, painting pictures, getting them to think bigger. Offering ideas outside the scope of his own services. *Leading* the prospect by effectively framing the conversation.

The sales pro is an Idea Generator, which is part of being a good salesperson. See the difference? The Idea Generator makes a very good living. The order taker gets by. Whatever type of freelancer you are, be an Idea Generator.

The reason I got hired by Dan Kennedy to work on the Proactiv campaign wasn't because I'm a brilliant copywriter (I'm pretty good, but there are many who are better). It was because I was able to generate tons of ideas, quickly, for how Proactiv could re-launch their product.

I dug into the research, conducted my own personal focus groups, and came up with tons of new angles for how they could promote their acne medication. It ranged from copy-specific ideas (many of which ended up in the final campaign in print, on the radio, and on TV), more emphasis on unexpected users (adults), and more focus on the emotions behind acne.

Could Dan have done this himself? Yes, and he did. But he also wanted the perspective of someone who was younger, and someone who had teenage kids. He wanted fresh *ideas*, and I gave them to him.

Coming up with ideas that make someone money is a valuable service! Get good at it, and you can get paid quite well.

Now, when I'm talking about being an Idea Generator, that means strictly for paying clients right?

Not at all. I mean give away ideas *magnanimously*! Ideas are free. Give them away to *everyone*, prospects and paying customers alike!

For example, before I ever started the Copywriter Café, I was giving away advice and ideas for a couple years. I fell into it naturally after a few copywriters saw some articles I had written about freelancing. Before I knew it, I was getting emails and even phone calls (remember when people used to use the phone?).

I estimate that I gave away over 1,000 hours of my time from 2011 until 2013, when I started monetizing the Café. That's somewhere between $50,000 and $100,000 of my time, pro bono, based on what my copywriting clients were paying me at the time.

Was it worthwhile? Absolutely. I wouldn't have built a thriving membership site and coaching business if I hadn't.

Would I give away *that much* time again? No. When people start asking you, "Do you have anything we could buy from you?" you know you've waited too long to start charging fees.

You don't have to give away time, but I *do* recommend giving away ideas. Again, ideas are free! You can always come up with more.

Where do you give away ideas? In your blog. (You can't charge for that.) Regular emails you send out. (Usually can't charge for those either.) In a special report you offer on your website, which you probably can't *charge* for, but for which you'll get something even better—an *email address*.

I'm constantly giving away ideas to other copywriters, like domain names, business names, systems, processes, marketing ideas. We come up with things all the time on Skype calls. In addition, I have notebooks full of ideas I haven't written about yet, and about 500 index cards with ideas for future articles, social media posts, videos, or services.

For me, it's hard to relate when I hear things like:

"I'm all tapped out."

"I used up all my good ideas on the first 40 blog posts I wrote."

"I can't think of any more new ideas. Everything seems like it's been done!"

These are common objections I get from copywriters when I suggest they become an Idea Generator. In fact, I tell freelancers all the time that they should frame what they do in these terms:

"I solve problems and I generate ideas."

So, where do you get ideas from?

How do you become an Idea Generator extraordinaire?

One big way that I mentioned in Chapter Six: **read, think and talk to intelligent people**. I can't emphasize enough the importance of reading, observing, and analyzing, and reading *outside of your area of interest*.

Then "connect the dots." In other words, synthesize the information, put the pieces together, make connections. Just like your body needs physical exercise, your mind needs mental exercise.

Specifically, you need to exercise your "idea muscle" (a great term I first heard from *Choose Yourself* author, James Altucher) on a regular basis.

That's why I hang out in cafés so often (without my laptop or iPad, I might add). I go there to read, think, observe, make connections, brainstorm, and write. It's where I got the moniker "Café Writer" from.

By the way, there must be at least 100,000 writers across the planet (out of seven billion people) who write and hang out in cafés like I do. Why did none of them think of snagging the domain name "cafewriter.com"? How in the world was that great two-word domain name available? It's very easy to spell and remember. How did no one think of it before I did!?

Because people don't think! I do my best idea-generating in cafés, in the sauna (watch for the blog), and while traveling. I bring a notebook and pen wherever I go, or record thoughts with my phone.

Read, think, and find *your* idea-generating places. I do recommend a café and the sauna, as well as the gym, the shower, and on planes and trains. Even while sitting in airports. For some reason, whenever I travel I do a lot of writing, and inevitably come up with new business ideas for myself, clients, or other copywriters.

In fact, if you ever want to hop on a quick Skype call, we'll do some brainstorming on the fly. I'll ask you about your business and its background, what you're currently doing, what's worked, and what hasn't. I'll come up with at least three new ways for you to monetize your idea, and I'll maybe even come up with a new product or service name, tagline, or business name. For free! (I told you I give away ideas. Connect with me via email at steve@cafewriter.com.)

Become a problem solver and an Idea Generator, and you will start to rule your corner of the freelance world.

Chapter 8: Stay Under the Radar

Isn't The Bright Side a lot more fun and encouraging than The Dark Side? Way more fun and *profitable*. Especially when you put all 11 Big Ideas into play. We've established that you need to think ahead of the curve. You need to become an Idea Generator. What happens when you succeed at both?

Your star starts to rise!

And lazy freelancers will see what you're doing and want a piece of it. Be prepared for borrowers, copycats and outright thieves.

Remember, ideas are currency, ideas get you noticed, ideas build businesses.

The problem is, if you don't *protect* your good ideas, they might just help build someone else's business. Let me share a sad, cautionary tale…

Lindsay (not her real name), was a rising copywriting star. She had taken courses, apprenticed under an A-level copywriter for a year, and diligently practiced her craft. She got good at the art of persuasive writing. Smart and creative, she was a prolific Idea Generator, long before I started talking about it. And she took my advice and always tried to think ahead of the curve. She didn't want to follow some cookie-cutter system. Lindsay had more than copywriting ideas, she had *business* ideas. Good ones.

When she came up with the brilliant idea to bill herself as a "List-Building Specialist" (before a lot of copywriters started doing this), she was pretty excited. So excited and proud of her idea in fact, that she started telling people about it in another Facebook group for freelancers (not the Copywriter Café). She put up a post describing her business idea. Of course, she got the usual pats on the back and encouraging comments as expected. Feeling the love from her colleagues and peers, she decided to write a blog post about it, too.

That got a lot of attention and copywriters started sharing it. You can see where this is going, of course. Lindsay's business grew quickly. It wasn't long before she noticed copycats online. Other copywriters were encroaching on her turf. Not only moving in on the same exact idea, but in some cases, doing it *better*. Sharper-looking websites. Facebook ads popping up everywhere, driving viewers to their site. Affiliate partners promoting it.

And then there was one that hit *emotionally* more than financially. She saw a friend's name show up on one of these copycat sites, in the form of a testimonial as a satisfied customer. Ouch.

Lindsay made the classic mistake of blabbing about her great idea and early success.

A much better approach? **Stay under the radar.**

This goes for everything, not just big business ideas. If you discover a new process that streamlines your business, identify a hot niche, or find a new marketing method that works like gangbusters, don't shout it from the rooftops.

At least, not until you've had the chance to package it and profit from it by *selling* your system or method to other freelancers. Or until you've had the time to get far enough ahead of the competition.

Before that, **stay under the radar!** Keep your ideas quiet until they're fairly well developed.

So how do you completely protect your good ideas? Even if you're not sharing your ideas with peers and potential copycats, if you have any presence online whatsoever, people are going to see what you're doing.

Here are seven ideas to protect your ideas:

1. Tell your prospective *clients* about it, not your peers.

You don't need backslapping validation from fellow colleagues, you need paying clients. Stay under the radar by only revealing yourself to prospects.

Of course, online your competition can easily scope you out. There are all kinds of tools to reverse engineer your competitors' campaigns. This is one of many reasons I'm a big fan of direct mail—it's much harder for your competition to snoop on what you're doing.

2. Buy any related domain names.

In addition to cafewriter.com and copywritercafe.com, I own copywritingcafe.com, freelancermanifesto.com, thefreelancermanifesto.com, steveroller.com, stevenroller.com. (Don't be like Jeb Bush, who somehow let jebbush.com expire. It immediately got snatched up by Donald Trump.) Plus 74 others, believe it or not. I have plans…

For looking up domain names, I use register.com. To actually buy them, I've used godaddy.com since 2003 and I've been very happy with them. I do use a different company to host my websites.

3. Give processes, systems and methods a specific name.

For example, instead of just describing my funnel system as a five-step funnel, I called it "The 5-Speed Business Accelerator," a term no-one had used before. If I saw it pop up after that I'd have my attorney send a cease and desist letter to the offending party.

Instead of calling my profit-generating marketing system something generic (like a "profit- generating marketing system"), I could call it, "The Wealth Pipeline," a term I haven't seen anywhere else before. Yes, at one time, I owned the domain name for that too. If you want it now, it's available, and could be a good name for the concept.

4. Take it one step further and use the ™ symbol.

You might have noticed I've used the ™ symbol a few times in this book, like after names of things I've come up with like Northwoods Plunge™ and Big Ideas Retreat™

It stands for "trademark," obviously, and you don't actually have to have a trademark federally registered in order to use it.

According to the United States Patent and Trademark Office, a trademark is "a brand name. A trademark or service mark includes any word, name, symbol, device, or any combination, used or intended to be used to identify and distinguish the goods/services of one seller or provider from those of others, and to indicate the source of the goods/services."

Key words here: "...intended to be used." If you come up with a great name for a product or service, start using it in print and *start using the* ™ *symbol.* And make sure you snag the domain name for it, too, of course. Protect your good ideas!

You can use the symbol before going through the lengthy process of registering the trademark. If you're going to use it long-term, it's probably a good idea to register it, though. *I am not giving legal advice here.* See an attorney, and read the discussion and watch the videos on trademarks at uspto.gov.

5. Register an official business name.

If you really plan to develop a concept or idea and it's going to be a core part of your business, consider actually registering it as a business name.

A few years ago, I started talking a lot about Big Ideas. I also knew I was going to get into publishing a lot of books and information products to help freelancers. It made sense to call my business "Big Ideas Publishing," and I went ahead and officially registered it as an LLC, a Limited Liability Company in the state of Wisconsin.

6. Get an official registered trademark or copyright.

Go that extra step I mentioned above and check out uspto.org for information on protecting your intellectual property. Again, I'm not giving legal advice, but it's not as complicated or as expensive as you might think.

7. Get an attorney.

Retain the services of an attorney who specializes in intellectual property law. Get one who's aligned with the values of entrepreneurs, freelancers, and small business owners. A lot of them aren't. Do your homework, and even if it pains you to pay for and associate with lawyers any more than you have to, it can save you a lot of headaches down the road.

Bottom line, **protect your Big Ideas**. *Stay under the radar for as long as you can.*

Chapter 9: Branding is the New Black

Now we get to my favorite big idea. I feel very strongly about this one, and firmly believe that people don't just buy your products or services, they're buying *you*. First impressions count.

I know a lot about branding. Or so I thought, until I met Desislava Debrova, the Branding Queen.

That's why I'm letting her write this chapter, the only one of 21 that I'm relinquishing control of. I trust her that much, and I believe in her business, her ideas, and her branding strategies that much.

Take it away, Des…

If you're reading this now…it's probably too late.

Actually, it's not too late for anything. I just really wanted to grab your attention, which, if you're still with me, I obviously managed to do. How did I do it?

I took a different road than most would, when somebody as awesome as Steve invites them to write a chapter in his book.

This, completely coincidentally (can people sense sarcasm through a page?), is how I've built my personal brand as well.

Let me ask you a question.

Say you're working as a social media manager, charging $8 an hour. Is it possible that in the span of two months, you can become one of the most sought-after brand strategists, charging thousands of dollars for your services?

Most people would say no.

Since you're here, reading Steve's book, you obviously don't feel an attachment to the word "mediocrity."

It is, indeed, possible. And I did it.

Oh, stop it—no need for applause. A few high-fives would suffice. Okay, maybe a standing ovation.

See, what I've always done throughout my career, is to take what everybody else is doing…and do the exact opposite. I love finding out what others think is impossible—and then just going for it. This, essentially, is what branding is all about. No, not necessarily being a rebel, but being *yourself*.

Instead of listening to people telling me my accent is a flaw I needed to fix, I went on and turned it into one of my biggest assets. Today, I'm speaking on stages all over the world and I can never imagine my accent would stop me from doing anything.

My Bulgarian nationality and the way I speak have become a big part of my personal brand.

Another thing—I've never looked at my competitors' pricings in order to work out my own. I've never seen somebody's PowerPoint and used the same colors and slides in my own.

Copying may get you *somewhere*…but it won't be where you want to go. I'm not going to drag you into the whole "be an original because nobody likes a copycat" cliché, but I am going to say this:

Value your originality. It's the one thing that will determine your business success. In a sea of people perceiving themselves as thought leaders when they've never had an original thought in their entire existence, **learn how to be yourself**. It's a strategy that always pays off.

Building a personal brand is all about knowing your purpose, identifying your core values and message, and positioning your brand in a way that makes you stand out.

If you're not carving your own path, but following someone else's...

Your brand will be a mere ghost of the person you really are.

Now that we've established this, it's time to get into the good stuff.

What the Hell is Branding Anyway?

I'm going to break the unwritten pact all brand strategists have and tell you exactly what branding is.

See, branding is nothing more than knowing your purpose and style and embodying them in every single action you take.

It's the process of expressing your brand values through every tool you have at your disposal: posts, podcasts, websites, social media graphics, presentations.

Remember Jeff Bezos?

He said "Your brand is what people say about you when you're not in the room." He's absolutely right.

Branding is all about owning a position in people's minds: a certain space.

Are you the badass brand strategist with the purple hair who always tells it like it is? Are you the kind and supportive life coach who breaks down health myths on a daily basis? Are you the hilarious copywriter who helps business owners implement humor into their copy?

Take out a piece of paper right now and write down seven things you want to be known for.

Here are mine:

- Bulgarian

- Grew up poor

- Nobody believed in her

- A passion for writing inspired by J.K. Rowling

- Not afraid to say the truth

- Edgy, hard-to- replicate personal style

- Has a sloth

If you look at my social media accounts, you'll see I consistently share stories that bring people back to these seven points.

This is so simple, yet barely anyone does it. Ever heard the saying "repeat something enough times, it eventually becomes the truth"?

It's quite accurate. Which is why you have a dangerous amount of power in your hands: remember, everything you share about yourself has to be true.

It shouldn't be what people want to hear. It shouldn't be a representation of who you want to be in the future.

Give people an accurate idea of who you are now…and use it to your advantage.

The 3 Biggest Lies of Mainstream Branding

One of the worst things about the entrepreneurial world these days is how many people are putting forth wrong information —with an insane amount of pride, at that.

Lie #1: Nobody cares about your story.

Let me ask you a question: when hiring someone, do you care about the type of person they are? Their personality? Character traits?

What's the best way to learn all of these?

The person's story.

As Nick Morgan says, "In a world where people have a lot of choices, the story may be the deciding factor." And it very often is.

95% of the people I've worked with have hired me or partnered with me because they heard my story.

I share it over and over again: on live video, on podcasts, in Instagram posts, tweets, and on my Facebook account.

It's emotions that differentiate a brand.

When you make people feel, you make people interested.

If there's something I want you to take away from this chapter, it's this:

People buy into you. Not your products, not your services, not your fancy visuals.

You.

The sooner you make your audience get to the "Wow! Now I get why she's doing this!" place, the sooner they'll start believing in your narrative.

It's that narrative that brings your entire business together. If you already understand this, you're five steps ahead of most people around you.

Lie #2: Always avoid embarrassing yourself.

It's only when you're ready to embrace embarrassment, that you'll be ready to build a powerful brand.

Bear with me here.

How do we get *really good* at what we do?

By failing, over and over again until we learn. By making embarrassing mistakes one after another, until we nail it.

When you're building a brand, you'll definitely make mistakes. If you don't learn how to deal with embarrassment—head on —you'll never feel confident exposing yourself and your business to many people.

I live stream every day. Every single live video I do, I have trolls coming in.

Trolls are people coming over to your video to throw negativity around in order to make themselves feel better about their lives.

When this happens, my audience has an expectation of how I'll deal with the situation, and this expectation is based on what they already know about me—about my brand.

The only reason I'm able to laugh everything negative off is because I've been embarrassed countless of times in order to learn how to deal with it.

Embrace embarrassment.

Lie #3: People already know me as _____, I can't change this now.

Remember my $8 an hour story?

Rebranding is possible in every single situation. It usually happens when the brand you've built is not aligned with your personality and goals anymore.

If this is the case, then you need to start changing your audience's perception of you in order for them to see the real *you*.

The only thing usually standing in your way is the impostor syndrome...which has no place in your life, considering how awesome you are.

How I did it:

- Changed my title from Social Media Manager to Brand Strategist
- Started pouring large amounts of free value about branding
- Used my master's degree in branding as leverage
- Indirectly announced my new pricing
- Said I'm opening spots for new clients

Obviously, there's a lot more to it than this, but the most important ingredient in the entire strategy is confidence.

My Theory of Ultra-Badassery

Before I say goodbye and leave the rest of this incredible book back in Steve's capable hands, I have another golden nugget for you.

One of the biggest things stopping people from really putting themselves out there and building powerful personal brands is the fear of others noticing their flaws.

This is where my theory of ultra-badassery comes into play.

To do this, you need to be self-aware...and you need to really own the things you consider flaws.

I know I talk too much and tend to get off-topic—which is why I always mention it to others. The key is to recognize something about you that is not generally considered good, and to be ironic about it.

This doesn't just immediately win you cool points—it also makes you more relatable to people. More vulnerable.

Have you noticed how everybody seems to be aiming for perfection these days?

Be a rebel.

Show your audience you're not perfect and show them the unpopular aspects of your character. Believe me... it will resonate with them. Ever heard the biggest cliche job applicants say when asked what their biggest flaw is? "I work too hard."

They do have the right idea in mind: turn a weakness into a strength. It's important to show self-awareness and vulnerability to a certain extent—and to always be strategic about it.

And remember...

Always value your originality. Even the things you consider flaws: they may just turn out to be your biggest asset.

Back to Steve...

Chapter 10: Stake Your Claim

In Chapter Eight, I advised you to stay under the radar as long as possible. At least until you can either package your ideas and sell them to the masses (including to would-be copycats), or until you've had a chance to get way out in front of the competition.

The best way to separate yourself from the herd and make your mark, is to Build Your Personal Brand. **Only you can be you**. People are buying *you* as much as they're buying your product or service.

Now it's time to plant your flag, set down roots, build your foundation, and stake your claim. This is when you shout from the rooftops! Tell anyone and everyone what you do!

This, I believe, is also the point at which you start transitioning from being a freelancer-for-hire to being a *business owner*.

A big difference between a freelancer and a business owner?

The business owner sets down roots. Lays a solid foundation. Throws down anchors that establish a permanent presence.

A freelancer doesn't have that sense of permanence. In the eyes of our clients, a business owner is here to stay and has developed a reputable image.

A freelancer is more of an unknown entity. While you may have long-term plans, freelancing gives off a subtle vibe that you might be here today, gone tomorrow. After all, freelancers do come and go. We've all seen it, right?

Since there's a low barrier to entry, becoming a freelancer isn't too hard. Building a business that *lasts*? That's hard. The good news is, since very few people do it, you'll stand out when you do.

So how do you stake your claim? How do set down roots as a freelancer and establish your turf, physically and online? There are 10 things you can do, and whether you're reading *The Freelancer Manifesto* this year or down the road in 2020 or 2025 or beyond, these 10 things will still apply.

1. Come up with a good name.

The right business name from the beginning is crucial. A good name is good marketing.

Your business name (and accompanying domain name) should be easy to spell and easy to remember. "Big Ideas Publishing" is pretty easy. "Café Writer" is easy to remember.

Do you like your business name? Do you like saying it out loud? Does it have a nice ring to it? How will it sound on the radio, or on a podcast interview?

Does your name indicate what you do? (It doesn't have to, by the way. Apple, Amazon, and Google don't, and they rule the world. You don't have the marketing budgets they had in the beginning, though, so choose wisely.)

Is it hard to spell? Anything confusing ("to" or "2")? Is it too long? (A common mistake I see.)

I've helped lots of copywriters establish their business name. I'm pretty good with coming up with names that fit these criteria, and good taglines to go with them.

When you hear a good business name, you know it. And we all know when we hear a bad website name, right? (Not mentioning names, even though that could be fun.)

What do you do then? Are you stuck with a bad name? Not at all.

It's a lot easier for we freelancers to change our names than big companies, that's for sure. Get a new domain name and start using it! Simple.

Also, consider using a central website as a hub. YourName.com (e.g. johnsmith.com) is a great way to go. I currently use steveroller.com to point toward an About page, but I'm either going to use that or steve.international (one of my 81 domain names) as a central portal for everything soon—my books, speaking, retreats, coaching, and Ecuador Excursions. Stay tuned.

2. Set up an LLC, S-Corp, or C-Corp.

Make it official. Yeah, you can go on operating as a sole proprietor for tax purposes, I suppose. But I can tell you that clients take you more seriously when you've taken the time to establish a company.

My Big Ideas Publishing, LLC makes me *feel* like I'm doing something much bigger, and I am. I had to grow into it, but I knew from the beginning that I had big plans for my business. If you do, too, why not go big and set it up right?

I don't know about other states, and again, not giving professional advice here. Seek out a CPA and an attorney on this one. But I know in Wisconsin where I live it was really easy to set up a Limited Liability Company on my own online. It only took me about 45 minutes and $130, and each year on the anniversary date it takes all of five minutes and $25.

For that I get tax benefits and personal liability protection, keeping my business and personal lives somewhat separate. For more information on this, check out sba.gov or legalzoom.com. I'm not recommending you use Legal Zoom to do it, but you'll get some answers there.

3. Bet on yourself.

What I mean is, go all-in! Go full-time if you can, once you have some regular clients and marketing systems set up.

I don't recommend jumping ship too early. Do you have a good job with good benefits in the New Economy? Keep it! Squirrel away some money little by little until you have 6-12 months of living expenses put away. Get some retainer clients on the side that you can service in your spare time (something I discuss a few times in this book).

But if you have an opportunity to go all-in and do this full-time? By all means, do it!

A lot of copywriters do this on the side, and it can be a good side gig, for sure. It's the same with real estate agents. A lot of them are part-time, and that's fine.

But think about this. If you're the client, would you hire a part-time plumber? Part-time lawyer? Part-time financial adviser? I know I wouldn't. I want someone who's all in, who's bet on themselves. Be that person.

4. Give yourself a professional makeover.

Like we talked about in Chapter Nine, first impressions count. Image is huge.

Get professional photos taken every year, have a good-looking, up-to-date website, and even consider a personal stylist. They're not just for women, by the way. More and more guys keep a wardrobe and style consultant on retainer.

Shakespeare wrote, "Apparel oft proclaims the man," and he was right. Mark Twain backed him up. "Clothes make the man. Naked people have little or no influence on society." There you have it.

5. Get crystal clear on what you do.

Not just what you do, but for whom, and how you're different and better, and what that matters. Start telling everyone (in your marketing, and socially when appropriate).

6. Find your first success story.

Case studies and good client stories are gold. Do a great job for an early client, write it up as a success story on your website somewhere, and you've got a foundation you can build upon. One story tends to lead to the next, and all you need is one to stake your claim and prove that you know what you're doing.

If you're a graphic designer, create a great logo and showcase it on your website. As a copywriter, I highlighted my first couple successful projects, and clients didn't know they were my *only* two projects up to that point. My wife, Emida, is a talented mural artist, and got her start in 2005 with a beautiful piece featured in our local Parade of Homes. That single-handedly launched her career and established her as *the* mural artist in this area. She staked her claim.

7. Let your clients do the talking.

Those client success stories are great to showcase. Even better? A golden testimonial from a satisfied client. Yeah, baby! Put those front and center on your website and wherever you can. Best, these days? A video testimonial from an enthusiastic client. Seeing is believing.

8. Put down roots.

Yes, even if you're a "digital nomad." That was a hot term back in 2014-15, not so much these days now that there are 80,000 digital nomads running around the globe, telling *you* how to be a digital nomad, too!

Some people would say I'm doing the same thing, I suppose. But I think from a client perspective, it's maybe better *not* to be constantly on the move. Or at least advertising that lifestyle everywhere you go.

I travel a lot, and I've spent a fair amount of time south of the equator, but my clients never know where I am. I like to keep it that way. I'd rather portray an image that I'm settled in one place, working diligently on their project. And from a purely practical standpoint, it's much easier to develop a rhythm to your work if you put roots down somewhere.

9. Let your light shine, more than just online.

Online-only businesses feel like they could go up in smoke at any time. Establish some physical presence, too. Speak, host live events, meet your clients in person if you can.

10. Write a MiniBük®.

This is one of my favorite ways to distinguish yourself! As they say at minibuk.com, these are "bite-sized books for busy people" and an "opportunity to publish a book that will help you cut through the clutter of digital overload."

A MiniBük® is a pocket-sized physical book that usually contains about 64 pages. Because of its small size, you only need about one-fourth the content you'd need for a regular book, so it's a great way to get your ideas out in book form before you have enough material for a full-length paperback book like this one.

You can also use them as a lead generator, a giveaway when you do presentations, or a pre-sell tool before a client meeting.

11. Write a book!

A book, a *physical* book, is going to outlast any social media posts, website copy, online courses, YouTube videos, or any other digital content you produce. Your clients and fans will hang onto a book even if they no longer visit your website. Writing a book is THE best way, in my book, to Stake Your Claim.

I actually came up with 40 reasons you should write a book.

1. You have important things to say, and the world needs to hear them.

2. People don't throw books out. Somewhere, 50 years from now, someone will stumble upon your book, read it, and act on it

3. When you're sitting on a plane and the guy next to you asks what you do, you can simply say, "I'm an author." Much easier than trying to describe what a copywriter is.

4. Same thing at social functions or cocktail parties. "I'm an author" creates more interest than "I'm a copywriter" or "I'm an Internet Marketer."

5. You'll get introduced to more people. Everyone wants to tell people about their friend, the writer.

6. If you're single, you'll get more dates.

7. If you're married, you'll have at least one person who thinks your book is the absolute best.

8. It will give you more credibility in your field.

9. You can autograph a book. Hard to do with an ebook.

10. Print is far from dead. In fact, according to a recent New York Times piece, ebook sales are slipping. (http://www.nytimes.com/2015/09/23/business/media/the-plot-twist-e-book-sales-slip-and-print-is-far-from-dead-.html?_r=0)

11. Ebooks don't make good gifts. Print books do.

12. You'll get you speaking gigs if you want them.

13. Those speaking gigs will lead to more clients.

14. People will start asking for your advice more, on all kinds of topics. This could be good or bad.

15. A book is much more effective than a business card.

16. One book leads to a second book. It's just the beginning.

17. When you send your book to a good prospect, there's a good chance it'll get their attention.

18. If you send it 2-day shipping via your Amazon Prime membership, your only cost will be the price of the book (and you'll get your cut of that).

19. Instead of always directing people to your website, you can tell them to check out your Author Page on Amazon.

20. A good Amazon Author Page could hook as many people as your website.

21. Amazon is taking over the world. Why not be a part of it?

22. You'll be able to develop programs and courses based on your book, bringing in more revenue.

23. You can get interviewed on podcasts, lots of people will hear it, and your reach will spread.

24. You'll get interviewed on radio stations if you want to.

25. Podcast interviews, radio interviews, and speaking gigs will drive traffic to your website.

26. Offer the first two or three chapters free on your website to grow your email list.

27. A bigger email list means more opportunities for selling your other products and services.

28. You'll be able to raise your fees on everything you offer because of your newly perceived expertise.

29. Remember your sophomore English teacher who gave you a "C"? Send her your book (if she's still alive).

30. If she's not? Send it to someone else who doubted your abilities.

31. Market it right and you'll have a nice, ongoing source of passive income.

32. Plan from the start to write a whole series of books. Think Robert Kiyosaki's *Rich Dad* series, or Tim Ferriss's *Four-Hour* books. If people buy one, they'll want each one in the series.

33. Bad at shopping for people like I am? Give them your book (autographed, of course).

34. Autographing your own book has to be one of the coolest feelings. I'll let you know.

35. I don't recommend this as a book-selling strategy, but can you imagine doing a book signing at Barnes & Noble?

36. Again, this isn't a strategy I'd recommend, but small, independent bookstores would be glad to have you do a short presentation and book signing for their members.

37. Helping an independent bookstore promote your signing will give you more practice selling yourself.

38. Promoting yourself will come in handy when you're famous.

39. You could become a New York Times bestselling author and make a lot of money.

40. More likely, you could become wealthy by parlaying your book into a business.

There you go. More on this idea of writing a book in my next book: *The Solo Sabbatical: How to increase your health, wealth, and relationships by getting away from it all.*

Be more than a digital guru or internet marketer. Stake your claim! Mark out the boundaries of your territory, online and physical. Tell your audience whom you work with and whom you *don't* work with. Make yourself slightly inaccessible. Working with you should be an exclusive thing.

Staking your claim is about **positioning**.

The last thing about staking your claim, this isn't like claiming your share of business that's out there before someone else does. This isn't about getting your slice of the pie before your competitors move in. That's serious "lack-thinking" and a scarcity mindset.

Going back to the economic discourse I had back in the Introduction and in Chapter One (and this should be my last economic reference), one theory states that the economy, or any sector of it, is like a big pie. There are all kinds of players, all scrambling for their "piece of the pie."

As freelancers, I believe we have a duty, an obligation to *expand* the economic pie. It isn't a fixed-size pie and we're all jostling, scrambling, and fighting for our share of it. No! We have the truly magical opportunity to expand the economy!

I'm dead serious about this, and I take responsibility for not only playing my part in that but in being an evangelist and spreading the word.

I am a freelance economy evangelist, and I will not rest, until my message has reached to the ends of the earth. My mission is truly international. I've already hosted one international event, "The Ultimate Writing Retreat for Freelancers," down in Quito, Ecuador, in June of 2014 and I plan to host many more.

In December 2015, I realized that 28% of my business was from outside the U.S., and my Copywriter Café group is made up of freelancers from 53 different countries. In fact, 32% of our group is from outside the United States. I mention this because I want you to realize that no matter what country you live in, you have a tremendous opportunity to stake your claim, and I'll do anything I can to help you.

By the way, my Copywriter Café group is not just for copywriters. It's for any freelancer who wants to use copywriting to build their business. Connect with me personally on Facebook or request to join the Copywriter Café Facebook group, and I'll add you to the group.

Bottom line: There has never been a better time to be a freelancer, to stake your claim, and to carve out a successful business than today.

And you thought *The Freelancer Manifesto* was going to be all dark and somber. Ha! The bright side gets even brighter, especially when you get good at a few key skills.

This is going to get fun…

Chapter 11: Get Good at a Few Key Skills

Remember way back at the beginning of this book? Time to revisit the opening three words in the introduction:

"Freelancing is difficult."

No matter what type of freelancer you are, running your own show is not an easy gig. It goes beyond mastering your field of expertise. You obviously need to be a good writer, copywriter, travel writer, technical writer, designer (graphic designer, website designer), coach (business coach, life coach, health coach), or whatever else you do as a freelancer.

That's imperative.

As we've discussed, any potentially lucrative business opportunity is going to have competition. It's the nature of a good free market economy.

So, first and foremost, you need to be good at what you do. Clients and competitors can root out a fake from a mile away. That's not to say you shouldn't get started getting clients and making money before you're a polished pro. You should. There are clients out there for every skill level.

What I'm saying is this. Your ability to thrive in your chosen field of freelancing depends in large part on your other core skills. You either have these or need to develop them:

1. Connecting skills

2. Selling skills

3. Marketing skills

4. Copywriting skills

We talked about these four foundational "hard" skills in-depth back in Chapter Three.

Now if you're reading this and you're a copywriter, copywriting is your main service, of course. You've got that one covered and I hope you're in my Copywriter Café Facebook group and in my membership site, cafewriter.com. If you're not in there yet and even if you're not a copywriter, I encourage you to join.

Not a copywriter? No worries, you can learn how to write adequate copy yourself, if you have a desire to learn this.

Buy a couple copywriting books on Amazon, soak up as much free information online as possible, practice, and get started with entry-level clients and projects. You don't have to spend hundreds and thousands on copywriting courses or conferences. Those things can help but they're not necessarily to write your own promotional materials, which we'll be talking about more in Chapter Fourteen.

Again, I don't care what type of business you're operating, what kind of a freelancer you are, if you can get good at marketing, selling, copywriting and connecting, you will out-perform and out-earn 98¾% of your competitors, guaranteed.

I've taught this at my Big Ideas business immersion retreats for the past four years. These are fundamental skills and essential to success. Freelancers sometimes ask me, "Which is most important? How would you prioritize learning these skills?"

Based on nothing more than my own personal experience and observational skills, here's how I'd order them and why.

Selling

Selling is number one, without a doubt. Even more than copywriting. You can hire a copywriter to write your ads and marketing messages, but if you're in business for yourself, you'll need to learn how to sell yourself and your services. You can have the best marketing and copywriting, and you'll still have to communicate with clients and prospects by phone or in person at some point.

Copywriting

Copywriting is number two. Again, as the founder of the Copywriter Cafe, I'm a bit biased. But even if I wasn't a copywriter and coach for copywriters, I would tell you that copywriting is a foundational skill. Whether you're a graphic designer, content writer, photographer, or any other type of freelancer, you should have some basic, solid knowledge of copywriting.

Knowledge of, and hopefully talent for (so you don't have to hire copywriters). No matter what marketing system you use, you have to communicate effectively. If you understand copywriting, you understand your audience.

Connecting

Connecting is third in my book. It's still about making a good first impression, finding ways to help other people, and developing authentic relationships, something that's sorely missing in the New Economy.

Two books I can't recommend highly enough: Keith Ferrazzi's *Never Eat Alone*, and the classic by Dale Carnegie, *How to Win Friends and Influence People*. If you did nothing else but learn and master the ideas in those two books, you'd be successful.

Marketing

Marketing. Marketing is important, but of these four skills, I believe it's the least important. Why? Because it's constantly changing. The other three are evergreen skills. Plus, you can always hire someone else to do the marketing for you. Not as easy to hire out the connecting and selling.

Some people think marketing trumps copywriting. I say, why not have good marketing *and* good copywriting? *And* know how to sell and connect with people. Get all four down, and you'll be unstoppable.

How do you know when you've developed these skills to an adequate level? And do you ever master them?

First of all, yes. I believe you can master them. Not necessarily the Malcolm Gladwell, 10,000-hour style mastery, or Robert Greene *Mastery* level, but with time and effort you can get partway there. I talk about this more in Chapter Eighteen, "Take your Business to Level 11."

And we've talked about these ideas throughout the book: Work on your craft. Think ahead of the curve. Become a Big Idea-generator, stay under the radar, build your Personal Brand, stake your claim.

While you're doing all that, simultaneously get good at selling, marketing, copywriting, and connecting.

"Wait a second," I can hear you saying, "I didn't sign up for all this. I just want to be a freelance _____."

Freelance graphic designer, freelance photographer, freelance copywriter, whatever it might be, they forget to tell you about these other skills you need, didn't they? ("They" being anyone who got you involved in your business, maybe had some program, tool, resource, webinar, or conference to sell you, but neglected to give you the *reality* of freelancing.)

Fine, you can be "just" a freelancer, compete with the masses, and blend into the background with all the other freelancers who do what you do.

Or you can become a "five-tool" player. A quick analogy and then we'll wrap up this chapter. I'm a huge baseball fan. If you are, too, you know where I'm going with this.

In baseball, a five-tool player can hit for power, hit for average, run fast, throw well, and field.

If you're a five-tool freelancer, you're really good at selling, copywriting, connecting, and marketing. In addition to those skills, you also know your industry inside and out. If you're a copywriter, not only are you good at copywriting, but you know who the other players are, you know where the gaps are, and you know what the supply and demand landscape looks like. You're a "competition sleuth" and know how to position yourself in the field.

One- or two-tool players may make it to the minor leagues but that's as far as they'll get. You can make a decent living playing Double-A or Triple-A ball.

But if you've come this far in your chosen field, why not go big? Why not hit the Major Leagues? It's there for the taking, and unlike professional baseball, I believe the competition is actually *less* once you get to that level.

Sure, you have to stay sharp and stay ahead of the young and up-and-comers. But life gets much easier, when you're a five-tool freelancer. As the surfers and skiers would say, *"Go big or go home."*

Even if you have the tools, there's one more thing you need. It's held many a freelancer back from making it big.

You absolutely need to...

Chapter 12: Develop Thick Skin

Develop thick skin from doubters and detractors, but also mentors and coaches.

As you start to make your mark and stake your claim in this big ol' Wild West, free-for-all freelance world, not everyone will want to see you succeed.

I guarantee you will have doubters and detractors. Doubters could be well-meaning friends and family, who think you're a little off for not having a real job. They'll say things like, "So, how's your little writing thing going?" or "I hear _____ is hiring. You should apply."

In most cases, they probably haven't had experience running their own business. Entrepreneurs and business people will usually be encouraging and supportive.

Detractors could be envious friends or colleagues. They could be your competitors who don't like you infringing on their territory. It could be past co-workers who don't like the fact that you "broke free to the other side." You may not even hear their barbs first-hand. They're likely talking behind your back, gossiping with their friends about you.

Look, you have to accept the fact, not everyone will like you. I know, I know, hard to believe, right? I can tell you, with a group of over 6,300 people, not everyone likes me. Usually they just leave the group, but sometimes they make waves.

Sometimes clients might not be happy with your services. When you're in business for yourself, the buck stops with you. Nobody to pass the blame to, up, down or sideways.

So whether it's family or friends who don't completely understand what you're trying to do, envious colleagues and competitors, or unhappy clients, customers, or followers, you simply have to develop thick skin.

Develop the ability to not let negative comments and criticism affect you. I've seen this wreck people. Seriously.

As you gain more attention, make more money, and become more successful, become emotionally resistant to any criticism that isn't valid. It's similar to the type of emotional toughness sales people deal with on a daily basis. I guess because I spent 17 years in direct sales from 1986 to 2003, this emotional toughness is a characteristic I've developed naturally.

Trust me, I've had my share of back-handed compliments, barbs, and sometimes downright bashing. Never to my face. People aren't that bold. No, they tell their friends, who then tell me (unbeknownst to the barb thrower). Yeah, I hear things. I realize I'm not everyone's cup of tea. You won't be either. That's a good thing.

Be yourself, build your Personal Brand, and realize that you will have detractors. Do what I call "applying the turtle wax." You know how when you wax a car and then it rains? The raindrops bead up and roll right off the car.

That's what you want to do with negative talk directed your way. Let it bead up and roll right off you, not penetrate through where it could affect you emotionally.

Ignore invalid criticism.

On the other hand, you actually want to seek out honest, constructive feedback. As freelancers, we work in a vacuum. We don't have colleagues in an office setting to compare ourselves to on our own. We don't have a boss.

Remember point number ten in Chapter 5? Not having a boss is *not* a good thing.

So, if we're not careful, we'll go on our merry way operating as a freelancer. We'll do okay financially, maybe even really well, but we won't tap into our full potential because we never got ongoing guidance, feedback, and constructive criticism.

What's a freelancer to do? By nature, a freelancer is a lone wolf. You're probably a freelancer in large part because you don't want a boss. Am I right?

Get feedback.

But you still need feedback on your work, or you're not going to improve nearly as fast as you should. You can get that feedback in the form of one-on-one critiques from colleagues and peers, a paid coach, a mentor (unpaid counsel), or peer reviews from a discussion forum in a Facebook group or private membership site.

They each have their pros and cons. Peer reviews are good because they're usually free, but they're usually also not as detailed or helpful. Critiques from a paid coach can be harsh, and possibly expensive. But that kind of deep, honest, and constructive feedback will usually propel us forward faster.

It's like the difference between getting help in a college Calculus class from the TA or professor versus the guy who sits next to you in class and understands it only as well as you do.

The problem is, harsh feedback can hurt. It's painful to realize we're maybe not as good as we thought.

You need to be immune to internalizing this kind of criticism. You can't take it personally.

But you should, by all means, seek out and listen to this kind of advice. Develop thick skin! And please, do everything in your power to get feedback on every aspect of your business on a regular basis—your website, marketing materials, sales copy, and your client work. For copywriters especially, it is imperative that you have someone critiquing your work.

Clients won't give you proper feedback. Family and friends are too nice. Peer review groups are often not the best evaluators. Seek out a coach and a mentor. I believe that getting a well-qualified coach or mentor who will work with you ongoing and in-depth, and not hold back, is the single best thing you can do to advance your business quickly. Bar none.

If that person is good, they will also encourage you to stretch and...

Chapter 13: Say "Yes" to Opportunities

Stretch

If I could offer one word of advice to freelancers of every kind it would be: **stretch**.

Stretch yourself beyond what you feel comfortable with. Stretch yourself beyond the bounds of what you've done before. Stretch yourself past what other people (maybe even including your coach or mentor), think you can do.

The typical modus operandi is to do what's required to make a decent living. It's not easy to push ourselves, especially when we're not accountable to anyone.

That's not me, though, and I know it's not you.

If you're anything like me, you decided to run your own show in part because you felt stifled within the confines of a traditional job setting. A job where your good ideas, hustle, and outworking your colleagues wasn't necessarily rewarded accordingly.

You're not satisfied with "making a decent living." You don't want to play "follow the follower" and do what every other freelancer is doing.

No, you're aiming for the big leagues, where the rewards are great, the competition is thin, and you can truly **leave a legacy** (see Chapter 16 for more on that).

What do you need to do? **Say "yes" to opportunities!**

Go out of your way to place yourself in situations where people will ask you to do things you haven't done before.

Say yes

Your job is to say "yes" to opportunities.

In a way, this concept of saying "yes" to opportunities is the story of my life. I never felt comfortable unless I was getting out of my comfort zone, to the point where I was often nervous and scared doing so.

The summer after my freshman year at the University of Wisconsin-Madison, I jumped at the opportunity to work with The Southwestern Company. I had no idea what I was getting into with this company based in Nashville, Tennessee. For 131 years, they had provided students a way to make money for college. Essentially, it consisted of going to the company headquarters in Nashville for a week of sales training, right after final exams were over in May.

After that, they assigned groups of about 20 to 30 students to various parts of the country, where we established a home base for the summer. We had to find our own place to live, pay all our own expenses, and then knock on doors 80 hours a week selling educational books door-to-door on straight commission.

Crazy? Slightly. A stretch? Most definitely. It involved serious self-discipline and serious skills.

(By the way, don't confuse this with roving bands of young people selling magazine subscriptions. The Southwestern Company is a very reputable company that's now been around for 162 years. Hundreds of companies look to hire students who have gone through this program, now called "Southwestern Advantage," a sales and leadership program.)

This job was so far out of my comfort zone, that most people who knew me were confident I was going to fail at it. It was a stretch, but I stuck with it. I learned how to sell, made some pretty good money at it, and came back to do the same work during the summers after my sophomore, junior, and senior years.

My best summer (1989) I made about $20,000 in 12 weeks, which equates to $40,071 or an *annual* income of $173,644 in 2017 dollars. Not bad for taking a risk and stretching, hey? I paid for college entirely by myself, graduated from the University of Wisconsin without a dime of debt, owned a car I paid cash for, and actually had money in the bank. Oh, and I also traveled to 17 countries before I graduated.

After gaining some selling skills with Southwestern, I thought I had the world by the tail. I was aiming big, planning to be a millionaire by the age of 30. My first real interview took place at The Plaza in New York City, with a legal publishing company called Matthew Bender & Company. It involved calling on high-powered attorneys in their offices, selling them law books and resources. For some reason I thought this would be a piece of cake now that I had some experience.

Wrong! No offense to lawyers everywhere, but there is no group of people I'd rather come into contact with less than them. I know this now; I didn't know it then. Even though I had a lot of successful selling experience, this was a whole different world. Corporate attorneys and executive secretaries (the "gatekeepers") in big high-rise buildings in Minneapolis were tough prospects to break in with, but I held my own and took my game up a notch.

Years later I discovered copywriting. Once again, like selling during college summer breaks and later selling to attorneys, this was a stretch for me. Even though I understood selling and was good at it, "selling in print," as copywriting is sometimes referred to, isn't the same.

Up until that point in my life, I had never really written anything. Two papers in college and they were both bad. Copywriting was a completely new skill for me, and I underestimated the amount of good competition I'd have. I studied the craft and worked at it for years in my spare-time while I was working full-time, finally making the break to pursue it full-time in 2009. I found out copywriting was the easy part. Finding clients was the hard part. No one ever told me, but I figured that out, too. Stretching, stretching, always.

After I figured out how to write copy and had a few clients fall in my lap, I had a couple opportunities to give presentations about copywriting. The first was to a group called Social Media Breakfast, to their chapter in Madison, Wisconsin. A friend of mine who knew I was a copywriter asked me to speak to this group, which turned out to be about 60 local business people on a Wednesday morning before work hours. She knew I was a copywriter, she didn't know that I was still pretty clueless.

Nevertheless, I put together a 60-minute presentation based on what I did know, and guess what? It was actually well-received, and I ended up getting a couple good leads out of it. Even though I didn't know much about copywriting and marketing compared to some of the A-list copywriting veterans, I knew more than a lot of the local small business owners, and they were grateful for the information.

Next, I had a chance to speak on a panel forum at a big copy-writing "bootcamp" in Delray Beach, Florida. I still wasn't exactly a copywriting rock star, but I did have some early success, and had a few nuggets of wisdom to share with my peers in the audience. About 300 of them, in fact. Talk about stretching! Once again, I wrote a good presentation, delivered it well, with a dash of humor even, and attracted the attention of some beginner copywriters who later sought me out for advice.

My point with all these stories? Most of my career, most of my *life*, I haven't had a clue! I never knew what I was doing, I simply said "yes" to any opportunity that came along.

What *did* I have? **I had drive and ambition and a willingness to put myself out there, even when it was uncomfortable**.

Here's what people may not know about me. Yes, I've given speeches in front of 300 of my peers and 60 local business people. I've been interviewed on the radio and for TV. I run a Facebook group of over 6,400 people and a paid membership site. I've given over 25,000 one-on-one sales presentations in my life, and carved out a great career in sales.

But I'm an INFP on the Myers-Briggs personality type.

"While they may be perceived as calm, reserved, or even shy, INFPs have an inner flame that can truly shine…INFPs often drift into deep thought, enjoying contemplating the hypothetical and the philosophical more than any other personality type. Left unchecked, INFPs may start to lose touch, withdrawing into 'hermit mode,' and it can take a great deal of energy from their friends or partner to bring them back to the real world."

I tell you this to let you know, none of what I do comes naturally! It all takes effort, and it's all very much a stretch for my normal inclinations.

Selling, giving speeches, stepping up and leading people—none of it came easy or naturally.

If an introverted, contemplative guy like me who would rather read a book alone at Starbucks on a Friday night than go to a neighborhood party can do what I've done, so can you. If you're willing to stretch.

Just a couple more quick stories, then I'll wrap up this chapter.

If giving a speech was a stretch, would running my own retreat be considered one, too? Probably, yes.

When I got into copywriting, the only events I saw were either big events for 300 or more people, with expert speakers giving kind of generic advice, or smaller mastermind events with maybe 40-50 people, also with guru speakers, but even more expensive. Both types were great for taking a ton of notes and "drinking from the fire hose," not so good for figuring out how to actually apply any of it and profit from it.

There weren't any small, intimate, personally-tailored retreat-style workshops at a reasonable price. So I created one. I started hosting my Ultimate Writing Retreats in 2013, a three-day event for anywhere from five to fifteen people, in out-of-the-way locations like Vermont and northern Wisconsin. They were a big hit, and as of August 2017, I've hosted 11 of them, all quite successful in terms of what attendees learned and the results they got afterward.

Prior to these retreats, I also conducted eight two-day copy-writing workshops for National Seminars Training. That came about because a recruiter saw "public speaking" on my LinkedIn profile. Once again, I said "yes." Did I wait until I was an expert? Did I wait until I was a million-dollar copy-writer? Nope. As Ray Bradbury was known to say, "Jump off a cliff and build your wings on the way down." I figured it out after I jumped, after I stretched.

Every opportunity I've ever said "yes" to in life has turned into something good that advanced my career. Working on my first $5,000 project, my first $10,000 project, working with the legendary Dan Kenndy. Writing this book (I'll let you know what I parlay this into in my next book, due out in 2018.)

Next? Who knows, maybe a TED Talk. It's on my list.

How does this apply to you?

There are five areas you should look for opportunities to stretch and say "yes" to:

1. Go for big client projects.

How do you do that? Start by creating a "Rolls Royce" service. If you don't have it, they probably won't buy it.

2. Network with people at a higher level.

I wasn't always comfortable talking to company presidents, marketing directors, or influential people like the Governor of Wisconsin (a couple years ago at the Governor's Mansion). But I've learned to be a good conversationalist, and anytime I've been invited to an event where I might be able to meet someone important, I take it.

3. Speak in public.

This, more than anything, will get you noticed and set you apart from your peers. I implore you to take advantage of every opportunity you will ever have to speak in public. Start small if you have to and work your way up.

By the way, I didn't start out giving speeches in front of 60 local people or 300 people from all over the country. I started by giving dozens and dozens of speeches at my local Toastmasters International chapter, the venerable *Risers from the West* in Madison, Wisconsin. I highly recommend Toastmasters to anyone who wants to get good at public speaking.

4. Host a live event of your own.

Nothing like playing event organizer, host, presenter, teacher, moderator, and coach all rolled into one to up your game in a big way, fast.

Whatever your area of expertise, I guarantee there is an audience of people who would love to learn from you, and would rather come to a live event than listen to you on a webinar or podcast.

If you ask me, a lot of people these days are hiding behind the monitor and the microphone because it's safer. I know lots of very well-known copywriters and marketers whose audiences would absolutely love to connect with them in person, and all they've ever done is online stuff.

I don't know if it's fear, laziness, or lack of organization, but there aren't many people hosting their own events. Some show up as a speaker at someone else's event, talk for 90 minutes, and head out. That's good, but not quite the same. Host an event yourself and you'll be able to leverage it into bigger things.

5. Write a book.

The Holy Grail! Easy for me to say, now that I have one, right?

Seriously, writing a book will put you head and shoulders above your peers. It's not easy to put together enough cohesive thoughts into an organized fashion that actually makes sense and reads well. When you do, you'll automatically be elevated in the eyes of your readers. They'll see you as more of an authority, and as I wrote in Chapter 10, there are 40 good reasons to write a book.

Besides writing this book, I've written a number of ebooks, and helped other copywriters with their books. I'd love to help you write yours.

With any of these five ideas, you will separate yourself from the masses of freelancers who offer the same service you do. It's very hard to do that when you're hiding behind your keyboard and only letting your online presence do all the heavy lifting for you.

As I've said before, to clients, we all look and sound remarkably similar, especially if they're only seeing our website. Be different. Look different. Do the things other freelancers aren't willing to do.

Get out! Put yourself out there! Let the world *see* you.

Chapter 14: Big Ideas + Copywriting Skills = Profitable Venture

By this point, I'm going to assume that you understand the value of copywriting skills, whether you're a freelance copywriter or any other type of freelancer. Copywriting is one of the four fundamental skills every freelancer needs to develop. We talked about this at length in Chapter 11.

Sure, you can hire a freelance copywriter. (They're everywhere!) For a lot of small marketing and copy needs however, you'll probably be better off being able to whip it off quickly yourself. After all, you know your business better than anyone else, right?

For bigger copywriting projects you outsource, having a good understanding of copywriting will help you direct any copywriter you hire.

This far into the book, you also understand the value of being an Idea Generator. Combine the two? You'll be unstoppable.

Here's what I mean. I already gave you one example, the guy from American Lantern Press. You might think, "Sure, he's a top-notch copywriter. Of course, he's going to do well." Top-notch copywriting skills alone aren't going to build a profitable business. You need the Big Ideas, too. In fact, you'd be better off being an Idea Generator extraordinaire with no copywriting skills than an A-level copywriter with no ideas of your own, constantly working for other people and helping *their* businesses grow.

This goes for anyone—copywriters, coaches, graphic designers, or any freelancer. Long-term, the value you create and the equity you build up in a business will be determined by your ideas, the copywriting skills you use to sell those ideas, and the marketing systems that incorporate that copy. We'll talk more about systems in the next chapter, Scale Your Business.

I've been hammering throughout this book that freelancing is *not* the ticket to wealth. Freelancing is *not* the same as building a business. Freelancing alone will get you one thing—a gig where you're constantly going from project to project.

There's a better way, and that's to create a business. A year before this book came out, I developed a detailed, one-of-a-kind program to walk you through this process step-by-step. *The 70-Day Sprint: How to go from unstable freelance income to profitable business owner in 70 days or less* is a giant guidebook that's meant to be done over the course of 70 days, one lesson per day. If you have the time to go through that, message me at steve@-cafewriter.com and I'll hook you up.

A few years ago, Gary Bencivenga, considered by many to be the world's greatest living copywriter, quit copywriting. He stopped writing for clients because he had a better idea: use his copywriting skills and a Big Idea to build a business.

Gary is in the olive oil business. It's something he apparently has a passion for, wrote a good website for (see freshpressedoliveoil.com), and created a subscription business around, which is brilliant.

No more copywriting for clients, even at the extremely high fees Gary commanded. Long-term, this looks like it will be a more profitable venture, and he's been able to take himself out of the equation. He has systems and marketing methods in place, great copy to promote it, and monthly customers. What's not to like about that?

In my Copywriter Café Facebook group, I have numerous examples of copywriters who have left the gig-to-gig freelance lifestyle in favor of using their copywriting skills and Big Ideas to build a profitable business.

Tanya MarCia had a knack for copywriting, but her heart wasn't in writing for clients. She realized she had the perfect client right in front of her: her husband, Fritz, a successful financial adviser. Using a combination of her copywriting skills along with direct response marketing and a branding campaign for Fritz, he's now one of the top advisers in New Mexico, if not the entire Southwest.

In a nutshell, if you like this idea, here are three basic steps (out of 70 days' worth of lessons):

1. Do an assessment of your skills or interests.

What do you do best? What do you do that others pay for (or would be willing to pay for)? What are you passionate about, that you could teach other people about? Think about how you can reach more people with any of those things.

2. Get out of the one-on-one trap.

Realize that as a freelancer, you can only work with so many clients individually. And not everyone who's a prospect for your business wants your one-on-one service. They may like what you have to say, and want some advice and guidance, but they may want to *do it* themselves.

3. Package it!

Package up your knowledge, ideas, and skills into a do-it-yourself (DIY) information product.

This could take the form of an advisory newsletter, webinars, online programs, membership sites (like cafewriter.com), ebooks, physical books, training programs, podcasts, or live events like conferences or retreats. I've done most of these, and I'm also looking at producing my own TV show. There's nothing like the power of a well-polished show people can watch, and not just the typical YouTube or live stream. I'm talking like a real TV show. It's in the works.

My point is that you can do any of these things. You can monetize each one. And you can *leverage* your business with each one.

A freelance business is severely limited by the number of people you directly can serve one-on-one. Aim for a *business*, a real business that builds equity and leverages your time, and grows into a long-term sustainable business that you can some day *sell*. How do you do that? Turn the page.

Chapter 15: Scale Your Business

A really big payday

Have you ever dreamed of a really big payday? I have.

In fact, I think about it all the time. I'm not talking about landing a really big client where you score $20,000 or $50,000 in one day.

And I'm certainly not talking about a rich uncle dying and leaving you an inheritance, or winning the lottery. Those two thoughts, common to many from what I've heard, have never crossed my mind.

No, I'm talking about a big payday where you sell your business and end up with a nice lump sum payout, in one fell swoop.

I have to admit when I first got into freelance copywriting in 2004, this concept was the furthest thing from my mind. How could you could build a business and sell it? You're working for clients on a project-by-project basis. Even if you have retainer clients, once you stop working, the arrangement is over. You're a hired gun.

Before that, I'd always been in direct sales. Unless you're an insurance agent who sells a book of business to another agent, you can't really sell your business as a salesperson either. You sell, you have customers or clients, but they belong to the company you work for. You get paid commission, and the company gets the ongoing client revenue. If you leave the company, that's the end of the deal. The company gets everything you built up, and you move on.

At one point, however, I got a taste of the idea of building and selling a business, on a very small scale.

An example

When my boys were young I started a side business called Nakoma Lawncare, LLC. I chose the upscale Nakoma neighborhood in Madison, Wisconsin, got business through direct response marketing (my first foray into copywriting) and word-of-mouth referrals, and built up a nice base of regular customers. They stuck with me, season after season, for a few years. Emida and I did most of the work, I hired some of it out, and my goal was to have a business to hand over to Alex and Solomon when they were old enough to do it.

Nakoma Lawncare was a profitable little operation, and would have easily provided either of them with a way to pay for college. But since neither of them really showed much interest in it, I decided to sell it.

Now, if I had scaled it bigger and implemented systems, with more customers and maybe a few employees, I could have sold it for six figures. As it was, I got a small five-figure amount for it and went on my way.

It got me thinking, though…could you use this same concept with a creative service-based business? Or could I somehow build an information marketing business and sell it?

What gives your business value

Then one day in 2014, the book *Built to Sell* by John Warrillow showed up on my doorstep from Amazon.

It blew my mind and opened up a whole new world of possibilities I never thought of.

I owe a huge thanks to my good friend, Leanne Rumsey, who sent it to me. For the first time, I realized that I didn't have to just be a highly paid freelancer. That's okay, but **so much more is possible**:

1. You can develop **systems and processes** into your business that *don't* depend on you and your skills.

2. You can build **a list of qualified prospects and clients** who are engaged with and interested in what you have to offer.

3. You can develop **a loyal subscriber base**.

All three of these things will enable you to build a business you can some day sell. You can't do those things if you're simply trading your freelance skills and time for money.

Let me give you two examples, one related to my small Nakoma business and the other related to my copywriting business.

After I sold my Nakoma business, I could have taken everything I had learned and implemented and packaged it up in an information product. I'm a pretty good writer, so I could have created a three-ring binder full of material on exactly how to start and run a lawn care business from scratch, with no experience or capital required. Either for guys who want to turn it into a full-time venture, or high school or college kids who want to make great money in the summer.

It's how-to, do-it-yourself information that could easily be sold via Facebook ads or other online marketing channels. Anything that you know how to do and other people want to learn can be converted, somehow, into an information product you can sell. If you're not sure how to do this, let's talk and I'll show you. Message me at steve@cafewriter.com, which you've gotten a few times in this book.

Pretty straightforward example, right? But what about a creative business, like a graphic designer or a copywriter? How do you package that up and sell it?

Well, John Warrillow gives one great example throughout the entire *Built to Sell* book. Buy it, read it, and internalize it!

Here's another. Let's say I'm a copywriter who takes a different approach than most. Rather than focusing on a particular niche, or focusing on me and my copywriting skills, I take a different tack.

I come up with a proprietary marketing system, specifically for helping small business owners who have both a physical and online presence. Part of my branding is that I operate my own little marketing and ad agency from a café (which I actually do, now). Since I run my agency from a café, and it ties in with the style of marketing I came up with, I call it Espresso Shot Marketing™.

The marketing methods and systems are different than what everyone else is doing, and very effective. They're also branded and memorable. (I'm not going to give you the details since I really am pursuing this.) Included in this marketing is a way for the business owner to engage their audience and sell more, something I call the Daily Espresso Shot. They also get Café Reports, weekly briefings from my Café Ad Agency that keep them abreast of what's going on with small business marketing, their competition, and the economy.

This is a marketing/ad agency/copywriting shop I can someday sell, and I'm going to. You can do the same thing with whatever your service is…IF you take yourself out of the equation, come up with some creative intellectual property (you can't just be John Smith Copywriting), implement some proprietary systems and processes, and build a base of loyal clients and customers. These clients need to be locked into the *business* and the *results*, not to *you*.

See the difference between building and scaling a business versus being a high-paid freelancer-for-hire? In one, you own the asset. In the other, you're a hired gun helping someone else build *their* business.

I've scaled a business and sold it before. I'm doing it again with the Copywriter Café, I have a few more ideas in the works, and I can help *you*.

Let's talk…after you read *Built to Sell*. I'll show you how to implement it for your situation.

If you do these things, and they could take a few years, you'll come to a point where people will see the value of your business. That's when you need to start thinking about something…

What's your Number?

What I mean is, what is the number, your dollar figure, you would accept if someone offered to buy your business?

How much would it take for you to walk away from your "baby," the business you poured your heart and soul into? The business you built up to a significant level? *That's* the number you should be aiming for and locked on to.

(For one of my businesses—the Copywriter Café—my Number is $1.5 million. I figure that will give me a little over a million after taxes and expenses to set aside for a rainy day. I have other businesses I'm working on now that I would then pursue full-time.)

Whatever your Number is, work backwards. Every business is different, but for some service-based businesses, the valuation is estimated at three and a half times annual revenue. (Businesstown.com has some good articles on valuing a business in more detail.) So, in my example, for my business to be worth $1.5 million, I'd need to have annual revenue of $428,571. It sounds a little more doable when broken down: $35,714 per month or $8,241 per week.

This is another big departure from the typical freelance model. I know copywriters who make $200,000 to $300,000 per year, but it's based entirely on their creative talents and brainpower. It's all dependent on them writing top-notch copy for big-name clients. If they stop, they might have $50,000 to $100,000 in royalties come in for a year or two, but very soon the pipeline runs dry. **That's not a business**. It's being a high-priced hired gun. Most people think of freelancing in terms of that model.

Think differently!

Figure out how you can implement marketing systems (which are changing all the time, and you can keep up with by being on my email list), processes, sales systems, and branding for the business that transcends your Personal Brand.

It may seem like conflicting advice, but it's not. In the beginning, as a freelancer, you do often need to grow on the strength of your personal skills and Personal Brand. Along the way, however, if you're going to scale a business and build something you can *sell*, you need to remove yourself from the equation. Take yourself out of it and replace it with meticulous and well thought-out processes for every step of your business.

Look at it like this—pretend you're going to actually *franchise* your business. Document everything the way, say, a FedEx Office print and ship center, would document all of its processes for franchisees. Create a "User Manual" for someone taking over your business, because at some point, someone will! (When their offer matches up with your Number.) In the meantime, this User Manual will help you stay super-organized, efficient, and productive.

Are you starting to see the possibilities?

This goes *way beyond* being a freelancer. I want you thinking really big. And I'm going to take a step back in the next chapter, take a step away from the pragmatic business side of things and get a bit philosophical.

Maybe it's the effect of ten weeks of hanging out by myself in coffee shops in Quito, Ecuador, writing this book. It's given me time to reflect on business, family, friends, and **my purpose in life**. I've had a lot of time to think about why I do what I do, the impact I want to have on others, and what I want to leave behind when I leave this world.

Chapter 16: Leave a Legacy

There's nothing like spending extended time by yourself. I love it.

Maybe it's a writer thing.

Yes, I fancy myself a bit like Hemingway, hanging out in cafes, thinking, writing. Unlike Hemingway, however, my drink of choice is coffee, not alcohol, and I'm not the master storyteller he was. Not yet.

I think we need to get away from it all to think clearly, generate Big Ideas, and structure them into some kind of orderly fashion so people will understand and benefit from them. The best way, in my opinion? Write a book! Obvious answer coming from an author, right? (Side note: watch for my next book, *The Solo Sabbatical,: How to Improve Your Health, Wealth, and Relationships by Getting Away From it All.*)

But you don't have to be writing a book to benefit from some time alone.

If you're building a business of any kind, I strongly recommend some kind of Solo Sabbatical every year. You can work on your business, lay out some plans, set some goals, generate some Big Ideas, and most important, consider your deeper purpose.

What do you want to accomplish? Why? Whom will it help? How? Will it last?

In other words, if you died next year, would people still be talking about you? Two years from now, will they even remember you? I know, kind of morbid to think about, and maybe deeper thinking than you want to go.

I think about these things, especially when I'm by myself.

Thankfully my wife, Emida, indulges me. I'm blessed. During my time south of the equator, she took care of our three kids who were all still in high school at the time (my oldest was already in college in New York City), and she held down the fort without me. While I missed Emida and the kids, I rather enjoyed the time alone and made the most of it. Yes, I'm weird.

I wouldn't necessarily recommend a 10-week solo trip like the one I took to Quito, Ecuador, to write this book. That's a little extreme for most people who aren't single, though it is good for the relationship, I'll tell you.

If you can, take a long weekend by yourself and maybe go to a cabin in the woods. You can get away, do some deep thinking, and take the first steps toward Leaving a Legacy.

What do I mean by leaving a legacy, and why is it important?

Can't you just make a ton of money, deliver a valuable service, cash out at some point and find a beach in Costa Rica to while away the days? Sure, nothing wrong with that.

But wouldn't it be much more meaningful to know that what you're doing has a greater purpose? That future generations are somehow going to be impacted by the work you're doing today? That you made a difference in the world?

Am I being grandiose and perhaps a bit sappy as a result of ten weeks alone with my own thoughts? I don't think so. I hope not.

A couple illustrations will help you understand what I'm talking about, and might help instigate a few ideas for you.

You're a _____ (graphic designer, copywriter, photographer—fill in the blank). Why do you do what you do?

Well, I'm a writer. I write because I have ideas I want to get out into the world. Ideas that are going to outlast me, and not float into the ether or "the cloud."

Do you think an aspiring business rock star 50 years from now is going to find an ebook of mine online and be moved to take a new approach?

I doubt it.

Or see one of my YouTube videos and make a change in their life?

Highly unlikely. "Ebook" and "YouTube" will be just as unfamiliar a generation or two from now as 45's and 8-track tapes are to today's generation, and just as inaccessible.

But books? Wonderful, glorious print books? I believe they're here until the end of time.

Print books are my chosen format to get lasting ideas into the world.

Sure, I'll use all the technical tools available to me to enhance my message. No doubt.

But the *ideas* are what I want to last. **The ideas we leave behind are our legacy**.

1. I believe the ideas and the effect of selling those ideas drive the economic engine of the world.

2. I believe that if we live in a free market, capitalist country that encourages entrepreneurship (like the U.S. still does, more than most countries), and that if we are reasonably intelligent and industrious, we have an *obligation* to become an even more productive member of society by getting those ideas out to the marketplace.

3. I believe that the more people embrace this philosophy of an entrepreneurial spirit, the more our economy will grow.

4. I believe that a rising tide lifts all boats.

5. I believe I've been given a gift of developing ideas, selling.

6. I believe I can help others develop those skills, too, and I intend to.

7. I believe that successful business ownership can lead to an amazing lifestyle of freedom, wealth, and adventure.

8. I further believe that a successful life in business will lead to better health and better relationships.

9. I believe that when all these things happen, there's a ripple effect that will spread around the globe, touching millions of people.

10. I believe that impacting millions of people starts with one Big Idea, written down in one book that influences one person to act.

11. I believe this book will do that, and I believe there's a reason you're reading it. (You knew there would be 11 "I believe" statements, right?)

My original purpose when I started the Copywriter Cafe in 2012 was to help 1,000 people build a successful business using their copywriting skills.

Now? **I want *you* to experience the abundant life like I have**. I'm dead serious when I say I want to reach *millions* with my message of The Bright Side of Freelancing.

What do you believe?

Will you take it to the next level, write it down in some format, and get it out into the world?

I hope so, and I'd love to help. That's one of the legacies I'd like to leave.

In doing so, I also intend to influence my kids (currently age 21, 18, 16, and 14), to adopt this entrepreneurial mindset. I want them to use their talents and gifts to benefit the world and honor the one who gave them those gifts, and to enjoy the financial rewards as a result.

God willing, I hope to live long enough to have the same influence on my grandkids. *That's* a legacy.

What about you?

Have you thought beyond your next client or project? It's not always easy when you're mired in marketing madness, caught up in the cash flow conundrum, and wondering about which way to go next.

Take a step back on a regular basis. Take a Solo Sabbatical for a weekend or an extended trip abroad, and think through these ideas.

When you figure out what you want your legacy to be, pieces of the puzzle will start to come together. And when you have a purpose and a plan that's bigger than yourself, others will take notice and follow along.

Let me give you two other quick examples of others who are thinking beyond the here and now, and already working on leaving a legacy.

My friend, Brandy Booth, wrote a book called *Unsocial Media Management for Business: The 'How-To' Guide for Managing Online Drama to Boost Your Bottom Line*. It's a great book designed to teach people how to turn negative situations into positive (and profitable) experiences.

He could have left it at that, but I asked Brandy what his bigger purpose was. "The legacy I'd like to leave is to help create a world where people focus on common interests," he said. "Instead of fighting and arguing and focusing negatively on one another, I want to see us focus on the collective big picture. We're all in this together trying to solve the world's problems."

Wow. A little bigger than "I wrote a book and want to sell a bunch of them," hey? Brandy has a meaningful purpose and a big "why" driving everything he does. I have no doubt we'll be hearing his name for years to come. Maybe you could negotiate a Middle East peace agreement, Brandy?

Another friend of mine, Sharon Olson, wrote a book called *Living Your Legacy: Change Your Story, Impact Your World, and Become a Visionary Leader*. Whereas I wrote one chapter on this topic, she wrote an entire book!

Sharon is one of those rare people who looks at the world and asks, "How am I going to make my mark?" In her case, through her book, through coaching, and by the way she lives her life, her legacy is helping other people make their mark. She's already done it with her family and clients, now she has bigger dreams to meet with world leaders and celebrities. Not as a star-struck admirer, but as someone who can help them live their legacy as well. Imagine someone like Sharon making it her mission to help other influencers in society? The ripple effect would be amazing.

I'm not overly impressed with too many business and self-improvement books out there, but I was struck by both of these books. Read them when you get a chance.

Real quick, two last thoughts.

This Copywriter Café business and the results from it are just one of the ways I hope to leave a legacy.

Besides helping freelancers like you develop a profitable business, I'm passionate about two other things in life, besides my faith and my wife. (Her first name, by the way *is* Faith. She goes by her middle name, Emida.)

One of my other business ideas, which you'll read about soon, involves a lofty goal of helping couples stay happily married for life. My aim is to play a small part in helping one million couples avoid divorce. I've experienced it myself and know too many people who have gone through the pain of divorce.

Can you imagine the ripple effect of one million couples who might have been headed toward divorce, making a choice to keep the romance and love alive and stay together for life? I believe this could impact families for generations to come.

Another passion of mine that you've probably picked up on is travel. Ever since I backpacked all over Europe for three months as a wide-eyed 22-year old, I've had a burning desire to travel the world.

I believe that when we experience other cultures, not just as a *tourist*, checking things off our "bucket list" (a term I really dislike), but as a curious, open-minded *traveler*, willing to adopt and assimilate to wherever we are, willing to engage and understand people wherever we go, we become more grateful and less demanding. We become more empathetic, more caring, more giving, and more of a citizen of this beautiful planet of ours.

Yes, I believe travel can do all that.

In short, **the more we travel, the more *alive* and more *human* we become**.

Imagine if we all worked toward that ideal? What a wonderful world it could be. With a couple of travel businesses, I hope to make a dent in this one too.

I want to leave a legacy of thousands of successful entrepreneurs, millions of improved and saved marriages, and perhaps tens of millions of global citizens who care more deeply about their fellow man.

Lofty ambition? Absolutely. Why not?

This is another idea where I believe the adage "Go big or go home."

You might be thinking, "I'm just trying to make a go of this freelancing deal. All I want to do is make a decent living, provide well for myself and my family, and some day have enough to cash out and chill. Do I really need to leave a legacy?"

No you don't.

I can tell you this, though. Since I adopted this final Big Idea, number 11, my life has taken on new meaning and purpose. Doors of opportunity have been opening left and right. Financially and otherwise, abundance is starting to flow. I believe it will for you too. **Leave a legacy**.

Chapter 17: Why I'm Burying "Freelancer" for Good

Congratulations!

You've made it through 16 chapters, including an entire Part I of The Dark Side.

You're still here, so I'm guessing my mini-rants and strong opinions haven't bothered you too much. (I sometimes hear from those who are offended. They're out there.)

Along the way so far, I hope you've gotten some solid core principles for building a successful freelance business. I've given you 11 Big Ideas for overcoming The Dark Side of Freelancing. (The Bright Side!)

I've had an amazing experience running my own business. From an economic standpoint the prospects for freelancers are only going to get better…IF you do things differently than most.

Use this book as an ongoing point of reference to make sure you do. As I mentioned in the beginning, mark it up, write in it, highlight it, let it spark ideas of your own, and jot down action items and goals you intend to pursue.

Up until this point in the book, I've used the terms "freelance," "freelancer," or "freelancing" 93 times.

Now it's time to bury "freelancer" for good.

I hereby declare the death of "freelancer" and all its forms, including "freelance," and "freelancing"! As Kevin O'Leary, "Mr.

Wonderful" on Shark Tank always likes to say, "You're dead to me."

"Freelancer" and all your forms, you are dead to me!

I will not be using this term anymore, except when referencing my book, which is a bit ironic, I suppose.

I have long despised the term "freelancer," but I was afraid to state my feelings publicly. After all, it's such a widely accepted word. Who was I to buck a standard staple in the business world, a big part of the vernacular, and the subject of countless books and blogs, many written by people I highly respect?

Well, forget all of that. I'm done with "freelancer" for good. It's buried. Out of sight, out of mind.

You don't have to jump on the anti-freelancer bandwagon with me. I'll gladly lead this parade of one, but let me tell you **11 reasons why I'm burying "freelancer" for good:**

1. It's overused.

If 40% of the workforce will be some kind of a freelancer by the year 2020, and I do believe the statistics, do you really want to be wrapped in with 40% of people?

How can that many people all be described by one word?

2. It's the antithesis of building a business.

We've talked this one…to death.

3. It implies "no structure, no organization."

I don't want to be associated with a loose business structure. Contrast that with someone who has a business name, proper business setup (an LLC, C-corporation, or S-corporation) and who operates according to the principles I've laid out here.

4. "Freelancer" includes the word "free."

I'm being a little facetious here, but I really don't like the unconscious mental association a prospect might have.

The client could be thinking, "Will Mr. Freelancer work for free in exchange for some "exposure" or promise of future work? Let me try."

Maybe that's a stretch, but I simply don't like the way "freelancer" sounds.

5. "Freelancer" isn't necessary.

Are you really going to refer to yourself as a freelancer? Freelance what? Freelance graphic designer? Freelance copywriter? Freelancer photographer? Freelance travel writer? How about just say graphic designer, copywriter or travel writer? It sounds much better without "freelance" in front of it. Life coaches and business coaches never call themselves freelance life coaches or freelance business coaches. Follow their lead. Call yourself what you are! Anything but "freelancer."

6. "Freelancer" is not a strong word.

It's inherently weak. It's like what you say when you're not completely sure of what you're doing and where you're going. "What are you doing these days, Lisa?" "Oh, you know, a little freelancing."

Typical reaction to that? "Oh."

7. "Freelancer" is vague.

It doesn't say much. The only thing it says to me is, "I flit about from gig-to-gig and haven't really found my place yet.

8. "Freelancer" says, "You can pay me less."

I'm telling you that from the perspective of someone who hires freelancers. I don't mind if they call themselves that, but when someone does, my first thought is, "You don't put yourself on the same level as a business owner. You probably don't have marketing systems that keep you booked up months in advance and you probably have little or no overhead, so I don't need to pay you as much."

I've asked other people who hire freelancers their impression of the word. I've gotten a mixed response and not everyone feels the way I do. It's just another factor to be aware of. "Freelancer" can be a silent signal that says, "You can pay me less."

9. "Freelancer" is ambiguous.

Ask ten people what the word means and you'll get ten different answers. In copywriting and Personal Branding, I'm big on specificity. "Freelancer" is not specific.

10. "Freelancer" is a lazy default word.

It says, "I wasn't creative enough to come up with something better." You're an entrepreneur, a business owner. You're probably otherwise a very creative person. *Show it* by coming up with something better than "freelancer"!

If nothing else, just eliminate it from the front of your title. As I said before, simply use "copywriter," "graphic designer," or whatever you are.

11. "Freelancer" is small-time.

You've gotten through 17 chapters of this book. I don't know you, but I have a strong feeling you are not ordinary. You don't follow the herd. You have big ambitions to use your talents and gifts to make difference, and to make a lot of money.

You are big-time! "Freelancer" is small-time. Leave it for others who don't have the drive, determination and creativity that you do.

I'm done for good with "freelancer."

My preferred terms? "Business owner," "entrepreneur," or simply whatever you are.

We're not even going to say "Rest in Peace" (R.I.P.) because I don't even hope that much for the term.

"Good riddance." How's that? Okay, I think I've beat this one to death.

Onward…

Part III: Your Abundant Future

In Part I, we went through The Dark Side. I showed you the reality of running your own business.

I talked about the 11 things no one wants to talk about. I dispelled the sacred cows that no one else is questioning. I painted a clear (and yes, dark) picture of what you're getting into and what lies ahead.

In Part II, I presented The Bright Side. Eleven Big Ideas to overcome The Dark Side of Freelancing. We closed it out with a funeral for a friend.

Part III gets even better. *Embrace* and *act on* the 11 Big Ideas: Think ahead of the curve. Become an Idea Generator. Stay under the radar. Build your Brand (it's the new black, you know). Stake your claim. Get good at a few key skills. Develop thick skin. Say "yes" to opportunities. Turn your Big Ideas and copywriting skills into a profitable venture. Scale your business. Leave a legacy.

Now...it's time to create your abundant future.

Chapter 18: Take Your Business to Level 11

If you've never seen this scene from the 1984 movie, *This is Spinal Tap*, search "level 11" on YouTube and you'll get it.

The movie is labeled a rock music "mockumentary," and it portrays the fictional British heavy metal band Spinal Tap. It stars Rob Reiner, who also directed, scored, and co-wrote the film. Reiner plays Marti DeBergi, the maker of the faux documentary.

In this classic scene, Marti and band member Nigel Tufnel, played by Christopher Guest, discuss Nigel's amplifier. It has a volume knob that goes up to eleven, instead of the usual ten, implying that they've taken things to a higher level.

Nigel: "The numbers all go to eleven. Look, right across the board, eleven, eleven, eleven and..."

Marti: "Oh, I see. And most amps go up to ten?"

Nigel: "Exactly."

Marti: "Does that mean it's louder? Is it any louder?"

Nigel: "Well, it's one louder, isn't it? It's not ten. You see, most blokes, you know, will be playing at ten. You're on ten here, all the way up, all the way up, all the way up, you're on ten on your guitar. Where can you go from there? Where?"

Marti: "I don't know."

Nigel: "Nowhere. Exactly. What we do is, is if we need that extra push over the cliff, you know what we do?"

Marti: "Put it up to eleven."

Nigel: "Eleven. Exactly. One louder."

Marti: "Why don't you just make ten louder and make ten be the top number and make that a little louder?"

Nigel: (pause) "These go to eleven."

Quick two-minute video break: bit.ly/SpinalTapLevel11

Classic. The phrases "up to eleven" or "these go to eleven" have become part of the general lexicon as a result of this movie, and even entered the *Shorter English Oxford Dictionary* in 2002.

The same year the Library of Congress deemed *This is Spinal Tap* "culturally, historically, or aesthetically significant," and the U.S. National Film Registry selected it for preservation.

So now you know the background for my running theme of "11" throughout this book! Ha.

How does this relate to you and your business?

Well, everyone else plays on a different playing field:

"On a scale from one to 10, how would you rate this?"

"10x your business." (Another expression I don't like.)

"He's a 10. She's a 10." (Can we blame Bo Derek for all this "10" stuff everywhere?)

Forget that!

You don't play by the rules. You eschew the status quo. You think ahead of the curve. Let others play the 1-10 game.

Take your business to level 11.

I want "11" to be an ongoing reminder for you that you should go about your business in a different way.

Throughout this book, I've given you tons of practical ideas for building your business.

Take Your Business to Level 11 is more of a mindset chapter.

I want you to wrap your head around the idea that success, huge success, can be yours.

We've laid the pragmatic foundation. Now it's time to lay down the proper mental foundation to create your abundant future.

Some of these things I've touched on at various points throughout the book. These aren't Action Items. You can't flip a mental switch and change your attitude about money, wealth, and creating a Level 11 business overnight.

They may not all resonate with you. A few of them might make you mad.

I hope they do.

I want to agitate your wealth mindset. Just like we slayed some business sacred cows back in Chapter Four, I want you to question common and conventional attitudes about business success.

This is a process, and if you're anything like me, you've come into it with baggage and biases that won't serve you well.

Here are 11 mental building blocks to build a Level 11 business. (You knew there'd be 11, right?)

1. Wipe the slate clean.

Wherever you come from, whatever your background is, regardless of past successes and failures, wipe the mental slate clean. Your past does not define you.

Develop a selective memory. I have very hazy memories of a 10-year stretch of my life. Not that it was that bad, I just choose not to dwell in the past, personally or business-wise.

Were you raised in a lower class household? So what? No one cares. Did middle class values and work ethic teach you to have a disdain for rich people? You better get over that one or you'll never become rich yourself. Wipe the slate clean as you embark on building a business.

2. Make a decision to reach level 11.

Some people really don't want to be super successful. They're content being average. It takes almost as much effort in business just to make it and be average. Why not give it a bit more and rise above the competition?

3. Don't put a premium on leisure time.

I've never understood the "working for the weekend" mindset (and now I can't get Loverboy's tune "Working for the Weekend" out of my head).

I get really antsy with too much leisure time. In 2010, I took the family to Florida for spring break. The kids were already world travelers, but they had never hung out at the ocean before.

It was fun, but after the first day I was like, "Now what?" I was bored and I couldn't relax.

Same thing with sporting events. I used to absolutely love watching baseball and football. I'll still go to one or two baseball games a year, usually with my dad, and it always brings back great memories of my youth. But I don't think I've watched an entire game on TV in years, not even the Super Bowl or a World Series game. I really get itchy with leisure time. I have to be doing something.

And golf? Again, great sport. I used to play a bit and I still watch the end of the big tournaments. But to spend three hours watching or playing a round? I'd go crazy. Leisure time is overrated.

4. Adopt a contrarian viewpoint of work.

My good friend, Ed Estlow always says, "I want to live my life so that you can't tell if I'm working or playing." I like that. Why can't *work* be fun? Work is my leisure time.

To me, writing a book is fun and that's part of my work. Writing an email message every day to my list is fun, and that's work.

Most people associate work with drudgery.

If you're doing something you don't like, I suppose it is. (And if that's the case, you're reading the right book.)

Growing up, I remember both of my grandfathers saying to me, "Don't ever work in a factory." One worked for the Kohler Company. The other worked for Bolens, making lawn-mowers. Good jobs, and they provided well for their families. But work shouldn't be tedious, boring, or routine.

Learn to *love* work!

5. Develop a keen sense of discernment.

What do I mean by this?

Become a good judge of business opportunities and the people involved in them.

The higher you go in business, the more people will start approaching you with opportunities. If the deal seems like it will be better for them than for you, walk away. If you don't get an immediate good sense for someone, stay away. If the opportunity seems to good to be true, it probably is. If the person seems a little too slick, proceed cautiously.

This may or may not be a mindset shift for you. If you're naturally trusting and look for the good in people and businesses, I'm not saying to become a cynic, but make a switch. Be aware that *you* have a lot to offer. Don't undersell yourself because you're eager to get involved with a potential client, business partner, or affiliate. Make sure the deal is as good for you as it is for them.

6. Avoid wealth haters.

It's an epidemic. The vilification of the rich has permeated every aspect of our society.

You see it everywhere. Politicians, news people, Facebook friends, TV, movies, everywhere. If you look for it and listen for it, you'll realize that vilification of the rich has reached epidemic proportions. **It is absolutely toxic**.

If you ever think or utter these words, you've already fallen prey:

"The rich get richer. The poor get poorer." "The rich don't pay their fair taxes." The expressions "filthy rich," "stinking rich," or "obscenely wealthy."

How in the world are you ever going to become wealthy if you carry these attitudes about rich people? What, are you going to become one of the greedy, evil rich?

It is *impossible* to achieve lasting wealth if you vilify the rich. Don't do it.

Go one step further. Avoid wealth haters all together. Their mindset and attitudes are toxic. Instead…

7. Study and learn from rich people.

Hey, here's a thought! How about instead of hating on rich people, *get to know some of them* and find out what they did to become wealthy.

Seek out people who built successful businesses. Invite them to lunch and ask them how they did it. Ask them for advice. Find out what they had to overcome to get where they are, and how they did it.

8. Start saying "Why not?" instead of "I don't think that will work."

Possibility thinking.

Look, I'm not trying to get all Oprah on you. I'm not a fan of The Secret or the Law of Attraction or any of that. I'm not at all suggesting that you can attract wealth with your mindset or attitude.

I believe in plain old-fashioned hard work, business systems, sales skills, and one law above all others: the law of supply and demand.

I'm talking something very basic here. You see successful people everywhere. Why not *you?*

It's not a matter of luck, being in the right place at the right time, inheriting money, or falling into it somehow.

In most cases, wealthy people got that way by hard work, great ideas, filling a demand in the marketplace, and persistence. If they did it, why not you? Find out how they did it.

One of my favorite TV shows is Shark Tank. It's proof that good ideas and an entrepreneurial spirit can triumph. Rich people are everywhere. Ask yourself, "Why not me?"

9. Keep a clear, sharp mind.

This one ties in with point number three. The same "work for the weekend" mindset seems to drive the "I need a drink" mindset. You've taxed your brain so hard all day at work that you deserve a drink to now dull it.

Where did this start? On college campuses, perhaps? College students think their minds are so overworked that they need to start the partying process on Thursday night to give it a rest.

Even more, when they come back from a month-long winter break and have two straight months of classes, they deserve a *real* mental break: Spring Break!

Okay, I got off on a little tangent there because I find the whole drinking culture in the U.S. a little ridiculous. I'm not a complete abstainer from alcohol. I'll drink a glass of wine if I'm a dinner guest and it's served to me.

My point here is a more general one. If you're going to succeed in business and become wealthy, do your best to avoid the leisure pursuits of most people, which include drinking heavily on the weekends.

Keep your mind sharp, especially in the evenings and on the weekends, when others aren't. It's a competitive advantage (which we'll talk about more in Chapter 19). Read. Think. Talk with intelligent people about intelligent things, especially rich people whose brains you can pick.

I'm not preaching here. If you enjoy drinking after a hard day's night, keep doing it.

My drink of choice? I think you know. Coffee! More than the taste or the caffeine, I enjoy the ritual of making it at home in my Bialetti Moka pot, and I enjoy hanging out in cafes for the ambiance.

Benjamin Franklin once said, "Beer is proof that God loves us and wants us to be happy."

I say: *"Coffee is proof that God loves us and wants us to be creative and prolific."*

10. Guard your time.

"Daddy, do you have friends?"

I'll never forget my daughter, Zaria, asking me that when she was seven years old. It was about a year after I started my full-time copywriting business. (I used to say after I became a full-time *freelance* copywriter. That word isn't part of my vocabulary anymore, as you know.)

To Zaria, it appeared that I didn't have friends. I did, of course, but I worked from home (still do) and I almost never had friends over to the house. What do people do when they hang out at home with friends? Watch football, drink beer, and talk about the weather. Three things I don't have time for.

I actually enjoy hosting people. Over the years, I've often had people even stay at our house for days, weeks or months at a time, but on a daily basis, I guard my time. You should, too, if you're going to succeed in business.

Don't be easy to reach. Don't answer the phone. Don't give too much of yourself. We talked about these things in Chapter Five.

You know I do a lot of my writing in cafés. The Sow's Ear coffee shop in Verona, Wisconsin, is my second office. I go there to work, not chit chat with people. When friends or acquaintances say, "Hey, we should get together for coffee," my first thought is, "For what? What are we going to talk about? Is this for business, personal reasons, or idle small talk?" I don't say that, of course, but if it's not for business, chances are I'm not going to have time for it.

If you plan to be wealthy, guard your time.

11. Be like Carnegie.

Andrew Carnegie was one of the wealthiest men who ever lived (second after King Solomon, and ahead of Bill Gates and Steve Jobs if you factor in inflation).

He once said, "I'm going to spend the first half of my life making money, and the second half of my life giving it away." And he did.

Carnegie was born in Dunfermline, Scotland, in 1835, and came to the United States in 1848 when his father decided to make a better life. They settled in Allegheny, Pennsylvania, near

Pittsburgh, where Andrew worked in a cotton mill for $1.20 a week. Later he worked for a telegraph company, then the Pennsylvania Railroad.

By the age of 30, Carnegie had amassed business interests in iron works, steamers, railroads, and oil wells. From there he built the Carnegie Steel Corporation into the largest steel manufacturing company in the world.

His philanthropic career started around 1870, and most people know him for his gifts of free public library buildings all over the world. When he married in 1887, he made his wife sign a prenuptial agreement stating his intention of giving away most of his fortune during his lifetime.

The Carnegie Corporation of New York, the philanthropic foundation he founded in 1911, has supported everything from the discovery of insulin and the dismantling of nuclear weapons, to the creation of Pell Grants and Sesame Street.

His essay, "The Gospel of Wealth," articulated his view of the rich as trustees of their wealth who should live without extravagance, provide moderately for their families, and use their riches to promote the general welfare and happiness of others.

If wrapping your head around becoming wealthy is still a challenge for you, be like Carnegie. Start thinking about how you can give it away.

You may think, "I don't need a million dollars. I just want to be comfortable." (News flash: Even a million dollars isn't going to last you the last 25 years of your life.) Or, "What on earth would I need $10 million for or $50 million?"

I don't know. You're right. No one *needs* that much money, but *someone* does. Some worthwhile non-profit organization that you feel passionate about would *love* to have one, 10, or $50 million.

So if you're still struggling with the concept of becoming wealthy, maybe you don't feel you need it, *deserve* it, or could even actually accumulate it, take the focus off yourself.

Make a list of causes that you would love to support more if you could. Start giving to them now at whatever level you can and keep increasing the amount as your business grows.

At some point, make it official. **Give it away**. Be like Carnegie.

Chapter 19: Outplay Your Competition

The phone call caught me off guard. *"This is Jane Steele (not her real name) calling from Los Angeles. Is this Steve? We'd like to review your application."*

Application, application…for the life of me, I couldn't remember what company in Los Angeles I had applied to. Then something she said hit me: Survivor!

Yes! A couple months prior, around June of 2001, I had submitted a video and an application to be on the TV show *Survivor*.

I had been a huge fan since the show premiered the year before, and I still am. It's considered the leader of reality TV because it was the first highly rated and profitable reality show on broadcast television in the U.S. The 35th season of Survivor starts in September of 2017.

The premise is great, isn't it? People from all different backgrounds come together to both work with each other and compete against each other. Each season takes place in a remote, exotic, usually warm location, which is part of the appeal to me. (I'd go to any of these spots, like Vanuatu or the Cook Islands, if I could go by myself and write my next book. With 15 other people for 39 days? Nope.)

Players are divided up into two teams, and the teams compete against each other in a series of mental and physical challenges. But within each team there's another layer of competition. At the end of each episode, the losing team has to vote one of its own members "off the island."

So while they have to work together as a team to beat the other team, they also have to work well within their group. They have to be strong, smart, and likable. They have to be a good teammate and good independently. Strong leadership skills are needed, without being intimidating or overbearing.

If you've never seen the show, it's quite interesting to watch the psychological machinations and group dynamics. Alliances are established, trust is gained and lost, and promises made and broken.

Kind of like real life, really.

The tagline of the show is "Outwit, Outplay, Outlast," and guess what? In the business world, we have to outwit, outplay, outlast our competition, too.

We haven't spent much time talking about competition because if you do all these things, you won't have to worry about it. As I've often said, the higher you go, the less competition there is.

Still, you need to acknowledge your competition. Acknowledge them, and come up with a plan to outplay them. Or squash them like a bug if you're ultra-competitive.

How do you do that?

1. Keep an eye on what your competitors doing.

Watch your competition without being obsessed with them or worried about it.

2. Revamp as needed.

Constantly be looking to tweak your own business model. The days of putting up a website, implementing a marketing system, and sitting back and watching the money pour in are long gone. Things are moving and changing way too fast these days.

We probably need to re-do our websites alone every 18-24 months or so, even if everything else is going well. Otherwise we risk looking like we're wearing last year's outdated clothing styles.

Much more often, we need to be making slight pivots and adjustments to our business model, playing off what the competition is or isn't doing. Again, without becoming obsessed. It's a fine line.

Less frequently, hopefully? A complete makeover or reinvention.

In any case, be aware of the competition and what they're doing right. Don't copy them and play "follow the follower," but play *against* them. *Outplay* them.

Besides watching for what they're doing right...

3. Look for gaps.

This is the part I love about competition (and why I still think I'd do well on *Survivor*)! It's easy to get into an "everyone's already doing it" mode and to feel like you're late to the table and can't possibly succeed because there's so many people doing it well.

But here's the thing. There are *always* gaps. There's always something they're not doing as well as they could be. Something their clients and customers aren't completely satisfied with.

And that's where *you* come in.

Take off your Personal Branding hat for a minute. Take off your business-building hat, your marketing hat, and your operations hat, and put on your *detective* hat. Become a super sleuth online spy whose main mission is to figure out exactly what your competition is doing right. More important, find out where they're missing the mark. It's pretty easy to do these days. Everything is there for the full-blown super-sleuth taking!

Where do you look? Online forums are a good place to start. Or look at their own Facebook ads (you should see the comments, even on good, solid Facebook ads).

Search "(competitor's name) negative comments" and you'll pull up some good stuff. Sign up for their lists. Get in their funnels, even to the extent of buying something from them to really see what they're doing. Check Facebook groups. Ask around. Dig.

The point is, even the best businesses are missing out on opportunities somewhere.

Quick example. When I started the Copywriter Café, I knew I wanted to get into the business of hosting live events somehow. I knew I didn't have the audience size yet to pull off a large event, and I didn't have the star power to attract gurus to a celebrity-style panel event.

But I spotted a gap in the marketplace. No one was hosting small, intimate events in a retreat-like setting. So that's what I did.

Since 2013, I've hosted 11 retreats with 5-15 attendees each. We've gathered in off-the-beaten-track locations like Minocqua, Wisconsin, and Vergennes, Vermont, as well as in more touristy places like Santa Fe and Chicago.

They've all been successful, and I have an online wall of glowing testimonials to prove it (see NorthwoodsPlunge.com).

These retreats are three days of intense, personalized focus on redesigning your business, complete with individual "Hot Seat" sessions, one-on-one and group feedback, and a solid game plan for getting fully booked within three months of the event.

My retreats fill a gap in between the big conferences or panel-speaker seminars and very expensive, guru-led mastermind events, neither of which compare to what I'm doing.

Not sure where the gaps in your space are? I can help. I'm really good at identifying what your competitors are missing out on. Message me at steve@cafewriter.com with "find the gaps" in the subject line and I'll see what I can do for you.

Next…

4. Don't hesitate!

You've done your homework. Your detective work has paid off. You've found the openings. Now what? Jump on it!

I see too many freelancers hold back at this point. Usually it's self-doubt. "Is this really a gap? Maybe there's no demand, and there's a reason no one's doing it." Or "Who am I to step in and fill the gap? What do I know? Is anyone going to listen to me?"

Disregard those feelings!

Get a second and third opinion from any trusted advisers (professionals in your industry, not family and friends) who aren't going to steal your idea. If you get a thumbs up or two, go for it.

Finally, if you're going to Outplay Your Competition, you absolutely must...

5. Develop a competitive spirit.

Not a cut-throat, win-at-all-costs mode, but a friendly attitude like, "I've got this. I'm good, no one else is serving this market, and I'm going to."

I can tell you this, from 31 years of being in direct sales and copywriting: Winning is fun! Finding a way to do something better than your competition is extremely rewarding. You help people get involved in something they otherwise wouldn't have, and you get compensated well as a result.

Fortunes are made this way. Yours can be, too.

I've given you tons of good tips in this book, way beyond the 11 Big Ideas to stand out and thrive in the New Economy.

But if I had to boil success in freelancing down to two things, it would be this:

Learn how to sell and develop a competitive spirit.

Business is fun, and it can be extremely lucrative when you learn how to sell well and when you develop a truly competitive spirit.

In the words of *Survivor's* tagline: Outwit, Outplay, Outlast.

Oh, and my plans to one day be on the TV show *Survivor*? Scrapped. I have something better up my sleeve. Emida and I are going to audition for *The Amazing Race*. Yes, I'm still competitive, and there's no one I'd rather hang out with on a reality show than my wife. Make sure you're on my email list (cafewriter.com) and I'll keep you posted on my reality show career.

Chapter 20: True Freedom and Your Powerful Future

There's no magic bullet. No quick path to online or offline riches. Well, there might be, but I haven't found it yet.

Building a solid, sustainable, successful business takes time. The overnight success stories you hear about? There's always a back story that's not as glamorous. You've heard the "I was down to the last $6 in my checking account and then I discovered the secret marketing formula" stories right? The true rags-to-riches stories involve a lot more than that.

I was going to call this chapter "True Freedom and Your *Profitable* Future," but you know what?

You will get so much more than a profitable business if you adopt and implement the ideas in this book.

Money is good. I love making lots of it and I'm sure you do too. The way I look at it, though, is that money is simply a natural by-product of what happens when you operate with integrity for the long haul.

Way beyond money and the wonderful things you can do with it, you will experience True Freedom and a P.O.W.E.R.F.U.L. Future when you put these 11 Big Ideas to work.

I think you'll get what I'm saying best with an acronym I came up with for the word "Powerful":

<u>P</u>eople:

The higher you go, the more you will meet cool people doing cool things.

Options:

Go to Ecuador to write a book? Why not? Take your 17-year old son to Greenland on a whim because he wants to go? Do it.

Worldwide Opportunities:

Take a year off to volunteer abroad (without having to rely on friends and family). Send your kids to boarding school…in Paris. Go with them. Develop business partnerships on continents you haven't seen yet. Stay in those people's homes when you go there.

Exuberance for life!

You'll experience seriously energizing vibes when you're in the zone, doing work you were called for.

Riches:

Not just material wealth. Good health. Sound mind. Happy. Fulfilled. Rich *relationships*. (*That's* what it's all about—relationships.)

Fun!

I can't think of anything more fun than immersing yourself in meaningful, productive work. Hobbies? I don't really have any. Work is my favorite! (Requisite *Elf* reference.)

Unyielding Faith:

Faith in the overwhelming belief that the plan that has been established for your life is a great one. This drives everything.

Love:

When you are doing work you love you're more fulfilled, you think clearer, you're healthier, your relationships are better, and you will have more love to give.

♪ All you need is love. ♪ Right?

Love and money…they make the world go 'round.

Chapter 21: The World Awaits

"They think you hung the moon."

Those words will stick deep in my heart for the rest of my days, and I'll never forget the way I felt when they were spoken to me. It was early September, 1989. I had just finished a summer of selling and leading an organization of 25 college students from the University of Wisconsin–Madison and the University of Illinois, working with The Southwestern Company.

I was 22 years old, I pocketed just over $20,000 in 12 weeks, and I was about to embark on the trip of a lifetime. A three-month backpack jaunt across Europe with my buddy, John Berkholz.

But I had a few things to wrap up first.

My sales manager, JT Olson, and I were hanging out at his pool in the backyard of his Brentwood, Tennessee home. Our little group of 25 students had been one of the top-producing organizations in the country that summer.

I had a boatload of money, which I should have been thrilled about. But the money took a distant second to the way I felt when I heard, "They think you hung the moon." JT was referring to a couple of the guys in my group who had expressed appreciation for the impact I had on their summer. Apparently I had said some things, led by example, and helped them with their own sales efforts. I wasn't even aware of it until he told me.

Whenever I wonder if what I'm doing is making any difference, I tell myself, "Remember the pool," and that memory comes flooding back to me. (If you're reading this, JT, thank you!)

That moment in time confirmed for me that I wanted to have a career in business somehow. Sales, marketing, coaching of some kind (not copywriting—it would be 15 years before I even heard that term). I knew the money would be good, and it has been.

More important, I'd be able to use whatever talents I had to have an impact on others. I want that for you, too. I don't know what your talents and skills are. I don't know if you're a copywriter, professional speaker, life coach, business coach, graphic designer, website architect, travel writer, blogger, or consultant.

No matter what your business, I can tell you this.

It's about people. It's about relationships. It's about your impact on the world. It's about "finding your grail." The money will happen. The other stuff? That's what really matters. That's what I want for you.

The world awaits your talents.

Make it happen.

Acknowledgments

"No man is an island..." wrote John Donne in 1624. While I wrote this book in solitude, 10 weeks alone in a studio apartment in Quito, Ecuador, I owe a debt of gratitude to a number of people for helping me get to this point.

Thanks to Ed Estlow for encouraging me, believing in me, and for being a sounding board. We became fast friends after meeting online back in 2011, and I've enjoyed getting to know you better ever since. Our ongoing chats keep me focused and moving forward.

To my dear friend, Tanya MarCia. Our meeting over breakfast way back when was the impetus for the Copywriter Café, and your advice and ideas are always spot-on. Thanks for everything you've done for me, and for inspiring me with the big things you and Fritz are doing in your business.

To Leanne Rumsey, you have given me so much business counsel the past few years, I don't know if I'll ever be able to repay you. Beyond that, though, your friendship means the world to me. Thank you.

To Kelvin Parker, my good friend, confidante, and business mentor. You have stretched my thinking, filled in my knowledge gaps (of which there were many), and connected me with opportunities I never would have had otherwise. You're also the best guitarist I know, and my non-copywriter friends think I know a bona fide rock star.

To Michael Beil, who took care of all the technical things I didn't understand in the beginning. Your passion for life and your faith are inspiring to me, and I'm proud to call you a friend.

To Cyndi Fine, who drew out a mind map for me on the back of a napkin at True Coffee in Fitchburg one snowy February morning. You had more of a vision than I could see at the time, and many of those ideas have come to fruition. Thanks for helping me with my first ever retreat, too, and for being a friend all these years.

To Dan Jones, my long-time friend, first-ever mentor, and all-around good guy. Thanks for your persistence in trying to return my phone call back in 1986. My life was forever changed as a result. I love you, man.

To Frank Monzo, the first guy who ever taught me how to sell. You have no idea what an impact you had on me. I thought you were larger than life when we first met, and I still do 31 years later.

To JT Olson, the man who gave me an opportunity to be a leader in 1988. That summer, and the following year, set the wheels in motion for my future. I wouldn't have gone into sales if it weren't for you, and I wouldn't have the business I have today either. Thanks for setting a great example for me in business and in life.

To Sam Horn, author of "Pop! Create the Perfect Pitch, Title, and Tagline for Anything." Thanks for spending an hour on a Skype call last year. You didn't know me at all, but you generously gave me your time, advice, and business wisdom. You saved me from a title for this book that wouldn't have worked nearly as well. Thank you!

To Gary Hennerberg, the copywriting and marketing legend. Your presentation on a Thursday night in November, 2008, at a conference in Delray Beach was my defining moment. You were living the life I wanted, and I decided right then and there that I would quit my full-time job within six months and dive headlong into copywriting. On March 30, 2009, I did. Thank you.

To Ed Gandia, a copywriter and coach extraordinaire. You may not remember, but on a phone call in August of 2013, I was on the fence about which direction to take my business. After talking for about an hour, you encouraged me to pursue coaching. It's been a rewarding path so far, so I'm glad I listened to your advice. Thanks for being a role model.

And finally, to my sister, Chris, for teaching me how to read when I was four years old. Thanks for playing "school" in the basement when we were kids. You got me started, and I've never stopped or slowed down since.

About the author

I blame it all on that one-way ticket.

It was early September, I had just made a pile of money over the summer, and I was ready for a serious change of pace.

My final semester of college would have to wait.

I did what any 22-year old with wanderlust and no responsibilities would do. I bought a Eurail pass, stuffed a small backpack full of essentials, and hopped on my first trans-Atlantic flight.

It nearly ruined me, in the best possible way.

Forevermore, I would never be able to go more than six months without an adventure of some sort. Those three months were a whirlwind of new experiences and non-stop thrills-a-minute as my buddy and I hit cathedrals, museums, and a pub or two across the mainland. We met interesting people along the way, and I made some lifelong friends.

We returned home, money gone, and I finished school.

My goal was to be a millionaire by the time I was 40, and since I already had sales experience, I figured that was the quickest route to riches. It could have been, and I did quite well.

But I was restless. I wanted to do my own thing, run my own business. Do work and life on my terms, not under some corporate timetable and structure. It was great business training, but too constricting and stifling for my tastes.

So while I never set out to be a writer, or a freelancer, I had no choice. If I was going to continue going on 22-year old-style escapades into my 40s and 50s, I had to make a change.

I did, and my life has never been the same.

Thankfully, my wife, Emida, has been on board with this plan from the start. She knew when we got married that I had big ambitions, contrarian ideas, and a rugged streak of individualism.

We're on the same page, actually, since she's a mural artist and operates a lot like I do. Imagine that, a writer and an artist, making a go of love and life! Cue the starving artist jokes here…yes, most people saw us on a straight path to the poorhouse.

It's been a wild ride, and we've had our share of ups and downs, but mostly up. We've taken our four kids all over the world, once to four continents in 48 hours. Most people take the requisite trip to Disneyland. We took them to Nigeria for three weeks, and Ecuador for an entire summer. They've seen us work from home since they were little, and they think everyone takes off whenever they want. We haven't had jobs since 2009, and we wouldn't have it any other way.

Today, I write marketing messages for some wonderful clients. I help other writers figure out how to run their business and make a good living freelancing. I write books, and I travel a lot, sometimes with Emida or the kids, sometimes alone.

Life is good.

I'm still madly in love with Emida, and two of our kids are now in college, two in high school. Not surprisingly, they're all freelancers in their own right. We have an actor, a dancer, an artist, and a teenage business mogul.

This is my story of how I made the freelance life work for me. Whatever your hopes and plans are, I know it can work for you, too.

Made in the USA
Columbia, SC
20 October 2017